DAY IS DAWNING

Bishop Otto Dibelius in East Berlin, June 1956

Day Is Dawning

The Story of BISHOP OTTO DIBELIUS
Based on His Proclamations
and Authentic Documents

THE CHRISTIAN EDUCATION PRESS

Philadelphia, Pennsylvania

Editor's Preface

THE AUTHOR of this perceptive account of the life and the labors of Bishop Dibelius has suffered abuse and imprisonment for his faith. It was in a subterranean isolation cell, where he was under persistent and ruthless questioning because of his religious activities, that he began to think about writing the Bishop's story. After his release he consulted many friends in the old world and the new. Encouraged and guided by their counsel, he set himself to the difficult task of giving the prison-born idea form and substance. Much of the writing was done in the United States.

His selection of incidents and his evaluation of events were continually checked with understanding consultants. The formulation of the story therefore assumed more and more of a team-work character, and the finished product represents a group assessment of the deeply significant period in the spiritual and cultural history of Europe covered by the life span of the Bishop of Berlin.

One feels, as he reads this stirring book, that both the author and the ecumenical churchman about whom he writes are saying to the modern world what Cyprian, saint and martyr, said in the waning days of imperial Rome:

We want to stand upright amid the ruins of the world, and not lie down on the ground with those who have no hope.

Those who were mainly responsible in the selecting of documents and the shaping of the story gratefully acknowledge their indebtedness to the American Council on Education, the professors of Luther Theological Seminary, St. Paul, Minnesota, and Richmond Miller, Associate Secretary of the Philadelphia Yearly Meeting of the Religious Society of Friends.

The title of the book was suggested by the final words of an anthem adapted by the poet and priest of the Anglican communion, Edward G. Marrison of Kuala Lumpur, Malaya.

FRED D. WENTZEL

Table of Contents

Foreword

In my relatively brief experience of ecumenical associations I have been in the presence of the Evangelical Bishop of Berlin on only three occasions.

The first was at Denver, Colorado, in 1952 during the Second Assembly of the National Council of Churches. He addressed the Assembly but I met him beforehand, having been one of those fortunate enough to be invited to a small private dinner where we had an opportunity to observe him at close range and in very intimate surroundings. His wife had died and been buried only a week or so prior to the Denver meetings but he kept his engagement to be with us there, for which we were deeply grateful since we needed so much the inspiration and insights which we had counted on him to give. His coming to us under those circumstances, however, with the shadow of bereavement still fresh upon him, lent an added cast to the legend of steadfastness which we had already come to identify with his name.

My first impression of him as he entered the little dining room that night I now confess was that of Prussian stiffness which in the American tradition had for so long been synonymous with Berlin and East Germany. But long before the dinner was ended I was convinced that, aside from a straight-spined military bearing which has come to be for some of us a symbol of his career as a witness for our Lord, what I had first mistaken for Prussian stiffness was really an imperturbable Christian serenity against which not even the gates of hell could prevail.

This revised first-impression of the Bishop of Berlin has been repeatedly confirmed and amplified during these ensuing six years. It has been delineated in even bolder lines by an unexpected gentleness of speech in his conversation and by a not infrequent twinkle of the eyes and a warm smile in which there is an element of constraint. The latter one tends to attribute to the uncertainties through which he has lived as much as to the nature of the man.

That imperturbable serenity to which these are appropriate accompaniments is strangely reminiscent of two of the sixteenth century Protestant Reformers whose traditions he so faithfully upholds. One thinks of Martin Luther standing before princes of this world as well as of the church and saying, "Hier stehe Ich; Ich kann nicht anders." And of Ulrich Zwingli as he lay dying on the battlefield of Kappel: "They may kill the body, but they cannot kill the soul."

Such serenity in contexts of this kind may be taken as the other side of the coin of Christian courage. It is that of men—Luther, Zwingli, Dibelius, and the nameless "innumerable host" of whom the history books record nothing—who are uncloudedly convinced that the word of the Lord as well as his mercy "endureth for ever." (Psalm 136 and 1 Peter 1:25.)

Most recently I was with the Bishop of Berlin in the summer of 1955. We were together at the meeting of the Central Committee of the World Council of Churches in the little Alpine village of Davos, Switzerland. He preached for us on Sunday morning, August 7, in the village's St. John's Church. That sermon illuminated and added to one's estimate of him as a man unshaken in his faith by the cataclysmic shocks of a revolutionary age.

His text was Acts 17:26, 27, and in his sermon it soon became clear that here once again was speaking, not a politician, but a

Christian churchman addressing himself to the life of his times from one vantage-point alone—the word of God and the church to which the proclamation of that word is now committed. He was scarcely launched into his sermon before he declared that "men are beginning to realize that it is the most vulgar and shoddy of all ambitions, to desire power gained by force, over others, whether individuals or nations."

One listened with the feeling that he was speaking to Washington and Paris and London and Bonn no less than to Moscow and Peking; that it was not the voice of an anti-Nazi or anti-Communist any more than it was the voice of an anti-Westerner except as it was a voice raised against any ideology or way of life which was anti-Christian and anti-human. This, it quickly became clear, was the Bishop's basic motivation. Human beings were, above everything else, not the faceless automatons of a state or an economic system or a political theory, nor the cause-less stuff with which personal ambition or cynical philosophy could deal lightly. They were, rather and always, souls for whom Christ died and precious in the sight of the heavenly Father.

"Make your welfare state," the preacher said later on. "But do not forget that there is a distinction between a hospital's being a repair-shop for the maintenance of a country's labor force, and its being a place in which care is given to the bodies of all the sick, whether they be young or old, rich or poor. Do not forget," he continued, "that it makes a difference whether the upbringing of the young develops in them a readiness to help those who are in need, or whether everything is left to welfare departments which have written over their doors: Please Deposit Your Souls in the Cloakroom."

He reminded the church as he reminded us churchmen from all over the world that Sunday morning that, when the peoples ask the great basic questions about life and history and the church attempts to answer, "she can answer only with the gospel, for the gospel is the only thing she has." And then, near the end of the sermon, as if he wanted to be first in aligning himself with the rest of us in an affirmation of that faith, he said, "There is One to whom nothing is impossible, and to whom we therefore pray that he may appear before the nations as he who can heal all the world's ills and put to rest all its questions. This One is called Jesus Christ. . . . Yes, the peoples ask, the church answers, and her answer is Jesus Christ, the Crucified and Risen Lord, praised in all ages."

It is such a glimpse of the man Otto Dibelius which enables one to understand what happened to him at Evanston, Illinois in the summer of 1954. That was the occasion of my only other association with the Bishop of Berlin. It is clear to me now, however, that when the Second Assembly of the World Council of Churches there elected him as one of its Presidents it was deliberately bestowing upon him the highest corporate honor, endorsement, and encouragement which it is possible for non-Roman, world-wide Christianity to bestow on a man at this time.

It was as if ecumenical Christianity was saying of Otto Dibelius: This man, as truly as has any other man on earth in our day, has stood for the right things, is heading in the right direction, is a trumpet giving forth no uncertain sound in recalling this shattered and fearful generation to acknowledge anew the Lord of the church as the Author and Finisher of its faith. We must let the world know, Evanston was saying, that he speaks the word which we know the church ought to be speaking, which the world desperately needs to hear although it is so sadly unaware of that being its real need; and we must lend strength to his hand and steadiness to his voice as he continues to bear this authentic witness to the eternal word of God.

His election at Evanston was Evanston's way of testifying that the Bishop of Berlin is the embodiment of moral integrity in a day when the Zeitgeist has ruthlessly taken moral integrity from the list of things by which men are assumed to live. The Bishop has steadfastly refused to call black white and white black just because it has become the fashion to act as if saying made it so.

It has made no difference to him whether the anomaly was uttered by a dictator with a short mustache or a long one, or by a white-tie-and-tails diplomat or statesman of the so-called

free world. It would just as surely make no difference to him
if it were uttered by a United States Senator. This churchman,
because he believes in God as the ruler of the nations and in
man as the child of God, will be found resisting both the "big
lie" and all the little lies which fertilize the soil in which the
big lie grows, simply because lies big or little do violence to God
and lead to violence among men.

Just as steadfastly, within the church the Bishop has insisted
that "our disunity as churches" must give way to "our oneness
in Christ." He has held to this position, perhaps most immedi-
ately, because the circumstances in which he has lived and to
which he has ministered have made clear that a world as badly
divided as is ours can only be made to hear the church's witness when that witness is spoken with a united voice. Moreover, it is apparent that the critical experience of the church in
the past quarter-century, especially in Europe, has confirmed
the Bishop's realization that the great confessional traditions of
historic Christianity, however necessary and worthy they have
been in the past, whatever the witness they have severally pre-
served for our good in the present, have always been possessed by
a unity more real than the differences which seemed to dis-
tinguish them from one another. They have all stemmed from
the same seed-root, "the root of Jesse" (Isaiah 11:1, 10; Romans
15:12) and all eventually converge on him again, acknowledging
Jesus Christ as Lord. This being true, the Bishop appears to believe, the churches are under perpetual imperative to translate
into the terms and structure of their corporate life the fact that
"ye are all one in Christ Jesus" (Galatians 3:28).

In all this Otto Dibelius has been in the forefront of what
is not so much a movement as a recovery by which the church
in the twentieth century has freed itself from a malady which,
rightly or wrongly but in any event unhappily, was believed to
derive from the pietism of the seventeenth and eighteenth centuries. Nowhere was that recovery given more dramatic and
precipitate evidence than in Germany, which was especially appropriate since it was in Germany that pietism was born.

Pietism, or what may have been only a partial and by so

much an erroneous perpetuation of pietism, acted as if the church could be true to its genius and mission by the steadfast cultivation of its internal devotional life through Bible reading and prayer, the performance of works of mercy and the establishment of hospitals and homes and other institutions to that end, but otherwise holding itself avowedly aloof from political life, the prevailing economic system, and international affairs as if all these were no legitimate concern of the church.

Such an assumption ignored or minimized several truths inherent in the gospel which the church was commissioned to proclaim—and practice as well. One of these truths presupposed the gospel to be unconditioned by geography. It originated in a simple, indeed primitive, society where an individual's relations with others of the human family were almost wholly confined within walking distance or the bounds of the village in which he was born, lived out his life, died, and was buried. But the gospel claimed for itself a universality so vital and dynamic that not only was it sufficient for the whole of man's life as man found himself in an increasingly larger world, but man in this larger world also had to live by the gospel—or die.

A second of these truths hinges on the fact that while man is not a creature of his environment alone, his environment does deeply influence his life. "Man shall not live by bread alone," the Master said, but he nonetheless recognized that the multitudes must be fed; and, as a wise teacher once remarked, "If he doesn't have any bread he will not continue to live at all." The so-called "simple" gospel originated in a social setting which was geographically small and where human relations were correspondingly simple, and in which therefore the church's pressing concerns were relatively few and also simple. But as man's world enlarged (or should we say it shrank?) with improvements in transportation and communication, the relations between men—in which God meant them to act as his children and therefore as brothers and sisters in the same family—multiplied in their number and became ever more complicated in their nature. The church, though it may have been slow in coming to recognize this, was under the same compulsion to bear its witness to this much larger and more complex world as to the little world in which the ancient prophets spake and in due time our Lord was born.

The Bishop of Berlin typifies the church's sensitivity to this compulsion. As a result, whether it is the issue of re-armament, or re-unification, or education, or the imposition of secular social responsibilities to the point where they absorb all of a people's time and energy so that there is no time left for the worship of God and service in his church—these are issues concerning which also the church must bear its witness even if at times it appears to be no more than a witness of protest.

For once again the word "protestant" takes on its full and proper connotations in a witness of this kind. Because it speaks *to*, and frequently *against*, certain conditions or proposals on which it cannot help but speak, the church sometimes labors under the handicap of seeming to be a characteristically negative institution with the word "No!" as its favorite word.

It is here that the ministry of the Bishop of Berlin has served to keep clear the true nature of the church's witness. There are times when the church says "No" but it does so only because it is the servant of that Creator and Lord whom Thomas Carlyle referred to as "the Everlasting Yea." When the church speaks, whether it says "Yes" or "No," whether it speaks words of judgment or words of hope, it does so only because there are some things to which the Lord of the church says "Yes" and some to which he says "No," and because the Bible, the church's charter and guide, is forever pointing it to the Savior who is alike the world's judgment and the world's hope.

The publication of a biography of Bishop Dibelius was long overdue. It ought to serve many useful purposes. Not least of all, it will enable many throughout the Christian world to come to know better one of whom they have thus far had only quick glimpses gleaned from occasional, though sometimes vivid, items in the news. Even these have contrived to make him for many a legendary figure who they have already come to believe stands in this troubled world for the things all followers of Christ should be standing for.

Even more important, the reading of this biography ought to illustrate and clarify for many devout souls who are not quite certain about it what it really means for the church to be the church, how the church must live in the world yet not be of the world, how it can speak legitimately and with power on secular issues the word which is a spiritual word because it is grounded in the Word of God. The Bishop of Berlin exemplifies the answer to these questions better at this moment than any Christian leader I know.

There is a three-fold sense of pride and gladness at the prospect of this book's publication. As President of the Evangelical and Reformed Church I am glad that one of the agencies of this church is privileged to be the publisher, because of the close historical and the fraternal contemporary relations between this church and the Evangelical Church in Germany. As an American Christian I am glad that an American church has a part in making this man's life and work better known to the world, and that gladness rises also from a realization that the Bishop speaks to America as meaningfully as he speaks to any other part of the world. As a member of the Central Committee of the World Council of Churches I am glad that at long last this heroic story of one of our six honored Presidents will be made available to the faithful of our ecumenical fellowship in more than 160 Protestant and Orthodox communions in practically every country of the world. This book should certainly be instrumental in binding us even closer together in the oneness which has been deepening ever since our organized fellowship began at Amsterdam in 1948.

The life-story told in the following pages will appeal to the more intelligent among those outside the church also, since the Bishop is more than a theologian and churchman as these have sometimes been caricatured. He is concerned for the live issues in a world on edge. He is deeply aware of the hidden forces of life behind each social and geographical frontier.

I shall never pick up this book or glimpse its title on my bookshelf without a grateful personal memory of the summer of 1955. I had talked with Christians of both East and West Germany and elsewhere as I traveled in central and eastern Europe. And then, during a long afternoon in Berlin—without the Bishop's knowledge of what was being done and contemplated —the possibilities were discussed and an initial understanding reached which bears its final fruit in the publication of this biography of Otto Dibelius, Bishop of Berlin, servant of the word of God.

JAMES E. WAGNER

DAY IS DAWNING

CHAPTER ONE

Born to Be Free

"KEEP ALOOF from public affairs! As a follower of Christ, you are not supposed to apply his way of life to the fabric of the present era. The Empire cannot grow into its fulness of glory, if ministers of the church continue to interfere with the processes of governmental action and imperial policy." So spoke the last Emperor of the Germans to one of the few pioneers who ventured to maintain the principle of the church's independence from worldly powers toward the end of the nineteenth century.

The man who interpreted those imperial words as an ill omen for Europe's destiny in the century to come, was Adolf Stoecker. He was called the Thomas Chalmers of Berlin, combining the rare virtues of a social reformer with those of an independent preacher of prophetic bearing. In the early nineties he regularly preached in Berlin's National Cathedral. But when he insisted that the sayings of Christ had significance for all people at all times, the aristocracy of the imperial court joined hands with some weighty banking concerns to make the Kaiser dismiss the "chaplain with the social leaning" and place all affairs of the church in a bondage that was even more obdurate than under Bismarck, the iron chancellor.

1

To be dismissed by the head of an all-powerful state-machinery has always meant a painful isolation for the nonconformist, a life spent in shameful obscurity. Hardly any law-abiding citizen would dare to speak to such an outcast, much less to listen to him. Reformer Stoecker, a man of deep social consciousness, sober and strong, had counted hundreds of thousands in his following. Not many of those enthusiasts, however, continued to follow him in the time of testing. Only a few of them kept the torch of freedom burning when darkness fell over the spacious house which had served as a parsonage and as a social welfare center in a city where the mighty were long accustomed to using power and prestige and privilege for their own ends only. Among those who remained faithful partners and fellow pilgrims on the chosen road to freedom was Otto Dibelius, an undergraduate student of history when Adolf Stoecker was ostracized and banished from his office.

Dibelius, just twenty years old in 1900, seemed in no way predestined to become a nonconformist. Son of a Berlin government official of good standing, nephew of a Protestant senior chaplain to a Roman Catholic Court, that of the ancient Kings of Saxony, young Otto's tough and daring attachment to a preacher of the social message added to the strange paradox of his early status.

Otto was the second of three brothers who were all nonconformists in their own ways. William, the oldest, thought the educational system of the state philosophers a flat denial of the dignity of man. In later years he was to be one of the reorganizers in the field of higher German academic training, successfully introducing modern principles of education as he saw them working in the Anglo-Saxon countries.

Francis, youngest of the Dibelius family, was an inspired artist before anything else, though he died as a soldier. A truly divine impulse moved him early to challenge a church which had become too orthodox and narrow in the presentation of the living Christ. To him Christ was the "loving brother of them that bear the burden of this transient life with a sense of expectancy and a love for the still hidden beauty of the world into which he came."

Whether greatness and beauty were to be painted on canvas, hewn in stone, woven in textile, forged in iron, voiced in rhetoric, or rhymed in verse, the three brothers of the Dibelius family were convinced that Christ, the prototype of man's perfection, should be envisaged as affecting every impulse and inspiring every craft of the human being. With this vision steadily growing within them, the gifted brothers found themselves confronted with a church that confined its program to propounding time-honored doctrines. These doctrines had some appeal to the elite who thought of man only as a rational being and were given to the glorification of intellect and reason.

In their neighborhood, however, the brothers saw ordinary people too. They were the people whose warm hearts prevailed over cold reasoning. They were the simple and the unsophisticated. They would take to their heels rather than listen to learned but shallow admonitions.

The first decade of our century offered a variety of opportunities to satisfy the hungers of the human spirit. Discoveries of science and revelations in nature gave wings to thought. To some these marvelous achievements of man seemed to promise the final fulfilment of a life gracious, warm, and colorful. With others who came of age at the turn of the century, Otto Dibelius felt a genuine hunger for that bread which endureth unto life everlasting. At the same time he could not but observe that there was no wholeness in the church; it had been split by elements alien to its very being; it had become the victim of temporal usurpers.

In a church established by law sophisticated speculations of thought were fatefully coupled with a perfectionist moral code. The functioning of the state and church relationship, which came to fruition in a showy and stilted squirearchy, provoked little enthusiasm from people like young Dibelius. The rising generation was tempted rather to seek questionable sources for the quenching of their souls' thirst. It was to the thirsty and hungry that the three nonconforming young men went out.

The second of the sons was originally to become a governing official in one of the principalities of the Empire, much in the traditional way. Traditional designs, however, did not suit him well. The study of European history and insight into the background of current events made him uniquely aware that the century which lay before him would be a period of global changes. Unless the atheistic teaching of communism was superseded by Christian solidarity in a fellowship of loving brothers in Christ, total war would soon bring about the end of ordered life on the earth. Unless the churches departed from their forbidding way of dwelling on the punitive side of God's interest in man, the remedy of a revolution more disastrous than that of France would be applied to free the peoples of Europe from the erroneous idea that state-machinery can achieve social harmony.

Other churchmen and more experienced people must also have been aware how completely surrounded they were by a state-machinery using covert ways of achieving its ends instead of open ones. But it was Otto Dibelius who, ten years before the first of our century's world wars, had the boldness to prophesy:

The century just opened will see a world-wide clash of the Christian and non-Christian forces. Whether Christ or his adversaries will gain the upper hand for a long time to come, will be decided in the middle of Europe.

CHAPTER TWO

Leader of the Youth

THE PLACE where Otto Dibelius chose to meditate upon the possibility of halting or sidetracking the world revolution predicted by the thought-provoking German Jew, Karl Marx, was Wittenberg, once the cradle of the Reformation. Where Martin Luther had nailed his parchment paragraphs, the ninety-five theses, to the door of the church so that both orthodox professors and inquisitive students should openly discuss them, there was now, in the first decade of our century, the cradle of another youth movement.

For two years Otto Dibelius had done research work in the field of comparative history of religion. When the University of Giessen in West Germany had rewarded with a Ph.D. degree his brilliant thesis on the attempt by Gnosticism to capture Christianity in the interest of Graeco-Oriental philosophy, the greatest academic dignitary of the time, Adolf von Harnack, encouraged him to become a professor at Humboldt's University in Berlin. A period of eighteen months was given to the young Doctor of Philosophy to choose between following Harnack, the liberal advocate of scientific evolution, or the less spectacular Stoecker who had too keen a faith to put up with any speculative theory of man's lifting himself to perfection.

The seminary student of Wittenberg was surrounded by an energetic crowd of young people confronted with the necessity of vital decision. Once more the town of Luther was the scene of two persuasions, the battleground of two conceptions of life that were incompatible with each other.

Four hundred years earlier the sensuality and pagan hedonism of the Greeks, then brought to life again by Italy's Renaissance, had been challenged by Luther's evaluation of the fallen creation and man's true justification by faith. A corrupt company of church leaders had been too complacent to see any danger for the souls of those exposed to various kinds of medieval superstition and wanton dissipation.

It was not given to Luther to see the Reformation completed. In European countries where the movement of Counter-Reformation set in before he died, the spirit of the Graeco-Italian Renaissance reconquered many provinces. The link between the morality of individual life and the ethos of public affairs ceased to be forged. There grew an easy feeling that politics could be kept separate from what the Bible says on human relations and community life. The pagan Greek conception of man being the measure of all things seen and unseen regerminated with the seeds of both Renaissance and Enlightenment. It culminated in France's "great revolution," which dethroned the God of the church and replaced his revelation by human self-perfection.

In the nineteenth century, Karl Marx succeeded in making the conception of the emancipated human being an operating principle in the movement for world revolution. The perfection of natural man was advertised in order to make men blind toward the monstrous atrocities to be committed in the interest of a world society in which all rivalries and class distinctions would be eliminated.

The great question as it appeared to Dibelius in his Wittenberg days was this: Would the drive toward world revolution capture the minds of young people in the more and more crowded cities of Central Europe? Would there be any alternative to that total war which was said to be indispensable in order to end war?

Then the more crucial question: Would the official heads and governors of the provincial Protestant churches be just as indifferent to the philosophy of world revolution as the Roman hierarchy had been deaf to the call for fundamental reform in Luther's early years?

In the twentieth century there were more fashionable faculties and larger seminaries than ancient Wittenberg could boast. Dibelius deplored the way in which graduates and undergraduates of the fashionable universities reacted to socialist trends among their nonacademic neighbors. Reformer Stoecker had not only been ostracized by the state executive; the great bankers of coal and steel concerns had also heaped ridicule on him.

Was it then to be expected from fencing and beer-drinking heirs of feudal times that they should leave their adventurous battlegrounds for the simple soap box of a prophet in the wilderness? It was Otto Dibelius' declared view that they should. As a prominent member of the German Students Association, he started the campaign against the noisy appeals to arms in what was traditionally euphemized as "affairs of honor," resulting either in resentment or in savageries extolled as "tender mercies." He urged his fellow students to vigorous thought and action:

To fight for the sake of fighting and to maintain that militarism or covert ways of enforcement are any solution to the social and international problems of Europe, is an anachronism.

To appraise force as a proper means for selecting the fittest of the human species is a denial of man's destiny.

We were created in the image of God and redeemed to regain the standard of cosmic design. We can actively help to redeem our time and our whole civilization.

With this great design for the perfect freedom of mankind, the divine Judge is the greatest revolutionary of all.

One of the texts Dibelius liked to expound to his fellow-fighters was: "If a man also strive for masteries, yet he is not crowned, except he strive lawfully." And his own words were:

*There is no statute promulgated in any state or common-
wealth so perfect and unchangeable that true followers of Christ
could afford to abstain from the process of amending the written
law from time to time.*

Real amendment of law, Dibelius believed, is basically also a
revolutionary act. It requires from the Christian self-command
in "striving lawfully."

Dibelius did not hesitate to tell his young contemporaries in
Wittenberg something quite unexpected about the transfigura-
tion of our inhabited earth, that momentous sound of the
trumpet which Christ's apostles forecast with fervent expectation. "The more urgently modern protagonists of the monster
materialism cry out for a revolution that would shake the foundations of a 1900-year civilization, the less will Christ tarry to
rise to judgment to help the meek and the humble on all the
earth." Such was his interpretation of the 76th Psalm.

Being aware how rapidly the idea of the Marxist revolution
was gaining in Central and East Europe, the growing disciple
who utterly disliked the dramatizing of happenings and obser-
vations could not help deploring publicly the "advised and
highly official indifference" to the undermining process on the
whole continent. His only comfort came from his conviction
that the great Judge to whom the ostracized and sometimes
martyred Reformers had appealed in all times of testing was
the same who had clearly stated that all law hangs on these
commandments: Thou shalt love the Lord thy God with all thy
heart, with all thy soul, and with all thy mind. Thou shalt love
thy neighbor as thyself.

It was at first surprising that a great adventurer in faith and
social action should begin the mobilization of latent forces for
a whole continent in a little town like Wittenberg. Yet it was
more than an outward coincidence that Europe's first Fellowship House was organized there (in 1905) on the basis of col-
lected dimes and quarters, without any state or state-church
support. It was most fitting then that this "House for People
Under Twenty" was opened and run by Dibelius when, at the

age of 25, he was a candidate for taking holy orders. From its very beginning, the House had a double purpose, retreat and social welfare center.

"To follow Christ is more becoming than to tread on the velvety smooth staircase leading to advancement in bourgeois respectability." With these words of Stoecker Dibelius refused a second offer of a university career. He was now fully convinced that the growing tide of class-war and universal hatred would never be stemmed by academic analyzing or experimental arguing. From deep meditation and continued intercession there was to emerge his own counter-action:

Those of the young generation to whom it may be given to love with all their heart, their soul, and their mind, will help to redeem the time, coveting earnestly the best gifts and being shown a still more excellent way.

CHAPTER THREE

Eastern Frontier

THE ATMOSPHERE of Greater Berlin in which the Dibelius brothers had grown up was brilliant in scientific accomplishment. Yet it was cold and apathetic toward the mystery of life, its uniqueness, and its beauty. In the highly industrialized city a "mechanically contrived togetherness" of business people and governing agents was unpropitious for what a true disciple of Christ associated with actual community:

The noise, the hustle, and the lewdness of the modern town makes away with the tenderness of true life, stabbing the very finest blossoms, wilfully frustrating their great potential.

The more prophetic task was surely to prepare a way in the wilderness. Soon after his ordination in the Advent season of 1906, Dibelius left the capital of the Empire for the east, taking a church in Crossen right on the edge of the Oder.

The Oder River had been for centuries the line from which western missionaries and knights in the service of the Church Universal had set out to prepare the ground for freeing Silesia, Pomerania, and the greater part of Poland from barbarian tribes invading again and again from Mongolia and the distant parts of Russia. On and beyond the Oder and its tributary, the River

Neisse, Christianity has always been fought for. The layout of borderland territory suggests the venturous character of the life of every successive generation. No legal establishment, no deed of warrant set up by the mighty is liable there to make the Christian's witness one of the nice and easygoing assets to traditional society.

Though most of the churches have been closed since 1945, printed copies of Dibelius' early sermons are still being circulated and read in clandestine prayer meetings. Among his favorite texts were these: "No man, having put his hand to the plough, and looking back, is fit for the kingdom of God" (Luke 9:62), and "He that is faithful in that which is least is faithful also in much" (Luke 16:10).

Here in the land of venture and youthful endeavor every little thing matters. Here in the frontier area our ancient folk songs are sung like hymns. Christian charity is unpretentious and genuine. One loving heart sets another on fire. Prayers are uttered in primeval fervency. Art is as colorful as it is simple. Garments are befitting and often very beautiful, but never redundant with circumstance or glamor. In our eastern borderland is an unchecked potential of true humanity, the rich blessing of those who are neglected and belittled by the power politicians fostering a colorless and classless society.[1]

East Germans have never been reputed for yielding easily or making compromises. When Catholic Austria expelled the Protestant Salzburgers from her domains, those who did not sail to Georgia in the United States found good work and happy homes beyond the Oder and the Vistula. The correspondence carried on between the freedom-loving pioneers of the German East and those advancing in America represents one of the most moving series of eighteenth century documentation.

In this virgin land of people who would obey God rather than men, divine revelation was not deprived of its unique signifi-

---

[1] From a sermon delivered by Otto Dibelius in wartime Lauenburg, East Pomerania; rewritten by the exiled Sisterhood under the direction of Adda von Kriegsheim.

cance by subtle attempts at subordinating the gospel of the
risen Christ to the relative standards of science and speculation.
In their brotherly sharing and in the profession of their fathers'
faith, the people living on their farm products and their weav-
ing industry between the Oder and the ancient frontiers of
Poland have been the most persevering of all Protestants in
Europe.

Heirs to the missionaries and knights of late medieval and
Reformation times, they had seen many fruits of their fathers'
labors reaped away by the Church of Rome in the nineteenth
century. When the twentieth century had begun, the question
was whether, in the face of a possible challenge from neo-pagan
quarters, the imposingly Catholic kingdom of Poland would
have the same inward strength as the German Protestants. The
latter group, more than any other in Europe, was keenly aware
of the first signs of planned subversions throughout the continent. So the problem that interested Dibelius in his Oder parish most strongly was this: Would the Roman hierarchy in Upper Silesia and Poland tend to compromise with secular powers
in order to safeguard their ecclesiastical status, or would they
eventually witness to the wholeness of the fellowship to be
formed by Christians of various traditions in order to keep all
Europe free from the horrors of a total war ushering in the
communist world revolution? These were Dibelius' words at
the time:

*I have no time to spend for any party moving in an anti-di-
rection, whether anti-Roman, anti-Polish, or anti-Russian. I
have come to realize that works of charity in honor of Christ
have been accomplished by a considerable number of Germans
who happened to be baptized and brought up in the Roman
discipline, mainly in our western parts.*

Dibelius was the first to bring home to his own national
church the fact that in the nineteenth century an easygoing coexistence with the rising secular powers had been more harmful
to Protestants than to Catholics. A far too liberal interpretation of God's design continued to strip the church of her sense

of nation-wide responsibility. The sacramental essence of the church had lost its impact on the daily life of Protestants.

With the Catholics it was still different. Their church consciousness, their keen sense of the corporate, had rarely given way to that boundless individualism associated with the agnostic world conception which appeared to the borderland pastor as the root of many hidden evils. In East Germany, Roman Catholics had assumed the function of a nonconformist conscience over against the more openly totalitarian tendencies evolving from the statism of the French Republic and two continental empires. Indeed, the Catholics maintained a moral and financial independence over state-church systems reaching from the Atlantic coast to Siberia in those imperial times. Yet it did not require Catholic training to sense that from LeHavre to Vladivostok all the cultural order was in ferment.

When the French Republic brought its separation of church and state into full effect, young Dibelius found himself at one of the farthest eastern outposts of German Protestantism. After serving in the United Lutheran parish of Crossen he was "promoted," rather surprisingly, to minister to a congregation of Reformed tradition in Danzig on the Vistula. This was a land of venture and challenge even farther toward the east. He went to Danzig's borderland Church of St. Peter and St. Paul, not for any leanings toward its Calvinist past, but for its very frontier situation.

In the Danzig area, at that time still independent from Catholic Poland, and even more along the Pomeranian coast of the Baltic Sea, it was already clear as daylight that the Christian community could maintain its vitality only if its members recalled the first phase of Christendom's long and varied history.

He who leads his daily life with Christ finds himself in the communion of the early confessors, missionaries, and martyrs. Theirs is the reality of the spiritual realm on earth unto this day. Outside their realm there is no abiding fortress, no continuing city. But to the city which is to come, there are signs and pointers at the wayside.

It is good and reassuring to find people who know how and where to erect those signs; they can help other people to find the narrow path to their radiant abode above.

The young pastor felt that in the historic frontier area he was very much among his own people. He liked their steady and quiet and warm response to his presentation of God's word. Just a century earlier, another Dibelius had written a hymn which the older folks now sang to him often. It was a simple but inspiring paraphrase of the 22nd Psalm in which the pioneers of Protestant Pomerania were boldly made to shine as the loving Father's birthright people:

> On earth our fathers hoped in thee;
> They trusted in thee, and thou didst deliver them;
> They called upon thee, and they were holpen;
> They put their trust in thee, and were not confounded.
>
> But as for me, I am a worm, a very scorn of men and the outcast of the people.
> All they that see me shoot out their lips and shake their heads, saying,
> He trusted in the Lord, that he would deliver him;
> Let him deliver him, if he will have him.
>
> They gape upon me with their mouths,
> As it were a ramping and a roaring lion.
> But be not thou far from me, O Lord!
> My praise is of thee in the great congregation.
> My vows will I perform in the sight of them that fear him.
>
> My seed shall serve him.
> They shall come and shall declare his righteousness unto a people that shall be born,
> whom the Lord has made.[2]

---

[2] The hymn by William Dibelius the Elder was written in the rich and romantic German of the early nineteenth century. For the reader in English, the words of the Anglican Psalter have been chosen.

Left, Otto Dibelius
at Evanston, 1954,
on the day of his
election as a Presi-
dent of World
Council of
Churches

Below, a verboten
assembly in Eastern
Saxony woods, 1953

Theodor Heuss, President of Federal Germany, and Otto Dibelius; Bonn, 1955

Presse-Bilderdienst

Opening of Kirchentag in East Berlin, 1951. Third from left: Martin Niemoeller. Fifth and onward: Otto Dibelius, Wilhelm Pieck, President of East Germany, and Reinold von Thadden-Trieglaff

Presse-Foto

How he loved the singing of their psalms and hymns and eastern carols! To worship with these people on the growing edge of Christendom was not a duty but a delight. No irksome air of listlessness among these people in their plain pews! Theirs was the music of the upper room, genuine and free from the forbidding sweetness, the luscious sentimentality of the super-civilized. How different this aspect of minority life was from the pageant and pomp of the imperial life of Greater Berlin.

When war broke out in 1914, four of Dibelius' children had been born in the east. The two younger ones were twin girls. Milk was scarce and heavily rationed. Extra portions could be obtained through connections with doctors of a certain standard of wealth. Pastor Dibelius had no such wealthy connections. So his twins, very frail in the beginning, had to drink a mixture of water and turnip juice, in rural Pomerania, the most agricultural of all German provinces.

The first world war brought disillusion to many Germans. Those who had flattered the King-Emperor with words of vainglory disappeared. They who had rested on the absurd saying that an empire like theirs was invincible under God were nothing but volumes of smoke. It was rather late in the day when the last of Prussia's kings realized what he had done when, in dismissing the Christian advocate of social and political reform, he had listened to the easygoing bribes of a religion unconvincing and yet established by law.

The man who had left the capital ten years before in order to trace the wellsprings of true Christian and true German life in the pioneer country of the east, came back to the city where he had been reared. The call reached him in the middle of the second world war. He had a sense of great historic changes still to come. Personally he was prepared to pursue the independent course of minority life which he knew would survive the breakdown of state religion and all its pageantry.

Resulting from the ritual and circumstance around the thrones of outmoded principalities, the number of state churches was as great as their denominational standard was striking. For over three centuries, the confessional allegiance of each prince had set the pattern of the individual subject's religion. In no other part of the world had preachers of the living Christ so long retained a system of subordinating religious persuasion and theological teaching to the decrees of "Christian princes and magistrates" as in Central Europe. Sprung from the sixteenth century defaults of Roman bishops, the system of churches established by emergency decrees has never enabled the German people, however virile and self-reliant it was from the beginning, to attain a moral responsibility in social and political affairs.

For a long time the sluggish dependence on princes merely fostered the assumption of man's self-sufficiency. Dibelius came to Berlin at the historic moment when masses of grown-up individuals were about ready to prove their own efficiency, waiting to take over from the representatives of an antiquated order. Being elements of modern mass society, they had never taken the opportunity of widening their class perspective by undergoing and partaking of a minority life. Nor had these young Marxists ever been to Luther's Wittenberg. They were proud of being quite a new type of German. To them the European background smelled of medieval or Reformation times. The considering of moral aims in the political procedure, the converting of religious emotions into everyday life was no part of their coarse training.

Had not Tacitus, the greatest of pagan historians, assigned a development of their own to the German race? Had not Nietzsche, among the prophets of secularism the most original, exclaimed that the God of the churches was dead and already replaced by supermen, the heroes of the Teutonic race?

The young pastor realized at once that the neo-pagans of Berlin had to be faced with the same faith that he had encountered in the Christian group in Wittenberg and in the greatly challenged minority east of Oder and Vistula where the Slavs were setting out to deny all Protestant rights and liberties. Dibelius came forward with the counter-question to be dealt with by Berlin's rising generation in the grievous aftermath of war and revolution:

Shall the aggressive views of a narrow nationalism gain the upper hand in Luther's country where the Reformation was once a blessing for all the world? Shall the pagan fallacy of a classless uniformity continue to be proclaimed without due respect to the historical past? Shall the new authoritarians prevent us from appealing to the historic fact that the Protestant heart of Germany, the middle and the east, has long been the driving power in the widening scope of the life of a continent which can still be seen as the most epic field of intercultural purpose and action? Who, then, shall deny that the course young Germany will take in her spiritual and cultural development is bound to have an impact on France and Switzerland, on The Netherlands and Scandinavia, on Poland and Czechoslovakia, and on our most powerful and strangely promising neighbors, the peoples of Greater Russia?

CHAPTER FOUR

Sunrise in Expectancy

IN THE FIELD of international relations, the system of exchange visits was a monopoly of professional diplomats until a long time after the first world war. The continental system of higher education was still so self-sufficient that a time for study and research abroad was regarded as a waste of energy or a sign of mental degeneration.

With his older brother, however, Otto Dibelius shared a healthful desire to breathe the air of a land where upright living had not given way to the complacency of the sophisticated, where the spirit of the Protestant Reformation had not been superseded by enlightenment or rational speculation on worldly issues. When a scholarship was granted for the year prior to his ordination, Otto Dibelius set out gladly for Scotland, to the amazement of the more conservative among his professors.

The personal admirer of Martin Luther had read about John Knox's witness too. From his studies on the Reformation he had a feeling that the Scottish Covenanter's rise against an authoritarian monarch was more congenial to the spirit of the Reformation than what he had experienced more than once on the continent: the watering down of Luther's spontaneous acts of faith by legal compromises with the powers that be. Doc-

18

trinal categories of orthodox flavor had too often served to
support those shoddy compromises.

In his first year at Edinburgh the youthful adventurer in
search of a full and genuine life with Christ came to realize that
the upright preaching of John Knox before Mary, the Catholic
ruler, was more deeply and widely recalled by the Scots of the
twentieth century than Luther's stand at Worms was recalled
in some provinces of western Germany where the Counter-Reformation had come in between.

The supporter of everything forthright and simple, the lover
of the unpretending, the honest admirer of natural beauty, the
scrutinizer of what was solid and undefiled in a nation's culture, the socially minded who was moved by such poetry as
"The Cotter's Saturday Night"—surely such a young man was
bound to be enthralled by the lowlands, the highlands, and the
isles of Scotland. It was the time when the second generation
of the Seceders, the new Puritans, was still alive. Many of the
lowlanders and Glasgow citizens had worked under Thomas
Chalmers, rightly called "one of the few real reformers the
nineteenth century produced."

The principle that in a country "reconciled with God"
churches should be free from any secular control and independent from state revenues, was operative not only in the disruption of Scottish Presbyterianism toward the middle of the nineteenth, but also in the first ecumenical event of the twentieth
century, the formation of the United Free Church in 1900. The
will to sacrifice earthly property for the kingdom of God, the
readiness to regenerate a nation without restricting the drive
of evangelism to what a state executive might think feasible
and fit for the "average" citizen, were striking features in the
development of that part of Britain which, in the words of
Ramsay MacDonald, has given its heart and soul to a commonwealth spreading over five continents.

Though in Scotland the Presbyterian Church remains a state-
connected church to this day, the free church principles of
Thomas Chalmers have come to be acknowledged all over the
country. The final reunion of 1929 has by no means resulted in

anything like the lowest common denominator, as often happens when church unions are brought about from outside. The reunited Church of Scotland is a national church in true harmony with the cultural ideals, the religious aspirations, and the global perspective immanent in the Celtic soul and expressed in Scotland's holy covenant to be an instrument in God's hand for the establishing of righteousness on all the earth.

Already in the Scotland of 1906, young Dibelius found the ideal of the interpenetration of the state with Christian life realized to an extent to which no other European country afforded a parallel. There were ruling elders, laymen of all classes, highly respected as the holders of a God-appointed office. Under the influence of Methodism, whose impact on the Scottish nation was to intensify through English channels, a host of catechists, relief workers, and lay preachers appeared to assist the pastor in the cure of souls and the ministry to the needy. With the support of the government, but with none of its neutralizing limitations, the work of missions at home and abroad, the whole range of humanitarian institutions, from the prohibition campaign to the provision for cripples and epileptics, were either subordinated to the church initiative or closely associated with it.

Secularism with all its pride and materialistic self-sufficiency, was no potent force here. Nor was it feasible to develop a rigid socialism along the eastern lines of class struggle and reckless anti-church activities. Here was a country where the transformation of the evil into an instrument of God's design was an undivided pledge. Whatever direction the movements of the century were to take, the pledge engraven in that rough and dour land of the north would forever remain a basic background reality. Dibelius responded to the pledge with a purpose lasting for a lifetime.

His home was still very much the continental borderland in the east. His ancestors had tilled the soil south of the Baltic. There his great-grandfather had been the well-known author of popular hymns in the time of Pomerania's evangelical revival. Yet it was a country where Christian liberty was still bitterly

disputed. Between the Oder and the Vistula young Dibelius'
pastoral work encountered utterly alien forces. Catholic claims
competed with the slogans of modern Socialists. Should it be
that either of those claimants would succeed in conquering the
soul of his beloved people, the Protestants of Germany's uttermost parts?

The first four years in the east were a time of deep searching
and grave responsibility. When he managed eventually to spare
a couple of months for a well-earned vacation he seemed more
than ten years older. For this second advance into freedom,
good fortune, and a festive period of thinking, the goal could be
no other than his first journey's end.

The year was 1910. A thousand missionaries from five continents were gathered in Edinburgh's Assembly Hall to rethink
the methods of foreign missions in view of the rising tide of a
neo-pagan nationalism in the Far East and Middle East. The
churches of Germany had not sent a single delegate officially
to this great meeting. Dibelius attended in a capacity almost as
strange and inconspicuous as that of William Temple, who
acted as a steward appointed by the Student Movement to help
in this humble way at a conference convened by the missionary societies of Europe and America.

It was here that Otto Dibelius met John R. Mott, the American Methodist and head of the World Conference Preparatory
Commission, and Joseph H. Oldham who was to lead the Continuation Committee and the subsequent International Missionary Council.

Oldham, a Scotsman himself, had studied at Halle in Central
Germany. Temple, by far the most creative of Episcopalian
youth, had been an undergraduate in Berlin and Jena. When
Temple later became the incumbent of two archbishoprics in
succession, he liked to testify that his "first acquaintance with
the world problem of an ecumenical church was made in 1910,
in the Assembly Hall of the Church of Scotland."

It is true that both Temple and Oldham had been reared in
state-supported churches. But they would not have chosen to
work with John Mott, had they ever favored the prearranged

patterns of institutional religion. Their new center of attention was the Far East with its very young churches. No time-honored Christian tradition existed in Southeast Asia. The experience of its peoples with the living Christ had still the freshness of a morning breeze.

To discuss the problems of Asia as major issues for the Christian message in a changing world was by no means the conventional thing to do in 1910. But if experienced young men like Oldham and Temple were anything but *Christians by convenience*, why should their new associate, the young messenger from Wittenberg, side only with custom and tradition? At least he would have to ask the challenging question how far the churches' tradition had become a static pattern, a glossy compromise in a situation too easily accepted. Deep in his heart he sensed how badly Europe's cultural issues needed clarification. And why should he walk in ancient shadows here in the country where the seeds planted by Thomas Chalmers were growing still?

Not in vain had young Dibelius been an ally of Stoecker, the defeated successor of Chalmers. Not for nothing had he seen how the reformer suffered from the unsavory fruits of ecclesiastical parochialism. By no means unjustified was his growing suspicion of the trends toward a planned society with their vigorous claims on the Christian conscience.

Though the leaders of the great Edinburgh Conference liked to look at the young Lutheran as a humble and self-effacing foreigner, this visitor to Scotland became deeply immersed in the wells and streams of the land in which Reformed Protestantism was still so much at home. In a country like that, the past was ever present. Such uniqueness of the historical scene as Scotland offered was magic to the young pilgrim from the land of holy knights.

A nation which pays little honor to its early fathers, is ripe for vitiation and unworthy to live on.

If he felt the past living and ever present in the missionary spirit of the Scottish Kirk, why should he not bring home to the continent the possibility of relating the past to history's present partners? Since Christ was the greatest of all partners in history, why should not ancient Europe be led to see the potentialities contained in her spring and early summer? If the standard which Scotland tried to live up to was a community of destiny outliving all materialist concepts, why then should his homeland fail to honor its history jointly with the forward movement to which God was inviting the world ever anew and never in an impersonal mass routine?

Surely the human mission of Christ could be confirmed by greater achievements than the nineteenth century had known. The twentieth century was still largely unwritten. However, a good inscription about its future way was in the making here in Edinburgh. With this inscription translated into German and French, a century more conscious of the historic church might overcome the tragic split between the reduced Son of Man of the liberal school and the unknowable Eternal which had become the ambiguous object of both the post-deist's reasoning and the enthusiast's emotion. Both of these philosophies of the nineteenth century were highly repugnant to a pilgrim in his holy enterprise.

Being somewhat nearer to the consummation of all centuries, might not the twentieth have been destined to work out a creative synthesis of human faith and human history, a joining of personal ethics and corporate achievements? Here in the north of Britain young Dibelius came to cherish the fervent hope that in the east a Christian century would be dawning too, and that a new generation would find a working relationship between the historic church and the rapidly changing world at large. Of such a relationship he saw the first fruits at the century's first great gathering in Edinburgh. With a feeling of admiration he sensed how greatly that working relation between church and world issues had already enriched the experience of the three witnesses he could not help looking up to. They were all present here in Scotland's royal city: Mott, the American, had labored in the Far East; Oldham, the Scotsman, in India; Temple, the Oxonian, in Southwest Australia.

Observing their various approaches and listening to all their
appeals, the young German observer could not find any word
more fitting for the reality to come than the term "ecumenical." The term had been used by the conveners of the first
Conference on Foreign Missions; it sounded very strange to
continental ears. Dibelius felt sure it would sound strange for
a long time to come. The German language would not quickly
absorb words so utterly ancient and Greek as *ecumenical* and
oikumene, meaning an outreach to the whole earth.

How flexible and heterogeneous the English language seemed
to the thorough German! What an advanced and seemingly
unruly form of speech it was, even in its slightly older Scottish
deviations! Whenever he discovered the Teutonic roots of British idioms, Otto Dibelius, much like his brother William, could
feel the ties of sentiment and thought-expression revived. He
literally traced and relived the movement of modern Britain's
Anglo-Saxon ancestors ravaging the Isles, dispersing the Celts,
and finally settling down to build a United Kingdom on German and Scandinavian foundations. He was thrilled by the
change of structure brought to the language by the Normans'
cultural conquest and the solid Saxons' happy intercourse with
the more Latin-minded organizers.

The English which the Dibelius brothers spoke almost exclusively for more than a year seemed more practical and functional than they would ever have anticipated on the continent.
This was no longer a captive language, no longer wholly at the
mercy of some deep-thinking individuals who replaced logic and
simplicity by an archaic richness of wording, no matter how
unintelligible the resulting phraseology might appear to the nations unaccustomed to German ways of thought and expression.

To young Dibelius the English form of speech appealed as a
means of collective and imperial communication. This was a
world language, and as such it was fascinating to the man whose
parish was ever widening for an ecumenical and truly pastoral
assessment of the whole earth:

You don't love your mother tongue, you cultivate neither its soul nor its spirit, before you have come to know and use other idioms, at least one foreign language often and well.

Language is a living unit, deriving its very life and growth from the fact that God himself has used the spoken word as a means to interact with man on earth. The genius of each language is derived from the greatest personal Being who took the divine initiative in speaking and appealing to man for a wholesome and sacred enterprise.

Now for an ecumenical undertaking, the first reasonable step was to make Central Europe appreciate the glory which was Scotland, the simple grandeur and cultural independence still maintained up here in the north. Shortly after the Edinburgh World Conference of 1910, Otto Dibelius went back to East Germany with a topical manuscript on "Christian Life and Work in Scotland" covering that country's mission fields on all the continents. The script was ready for publication, complete with statistics of a revealing and indeed a revolutionary impact.

Continental churches showed little readiness for any change. If a change was to come at all, ecclesiastical statesmen would hardly notice its challenge. The rigid and orthodox post-Reformation expounders did not have it in their Holy Roman Empire tradition to contemplate any phenomenon outside their established usage as having a global consequence to which they should pay attention. Returning from free and far-reaching Scotland, young Dibelius wondered if it should be the continued fate of his beloved homeland that here the spiritual remained subordinate to the temporal. Could that traditional way of subordination be justified from the scriptural basis now reaffirmed as the true foundation of corporate life?

Having reached the sense of Scotland's community and the better part of her inheritance, the valiant pilgrim made up his mind to exemplify in his further ways the full relation of the gospel to all of life, individual and corporate. He had as yet no ecclesiastical authority whatsoever. But outgoing and gaining ground was his inspiration to join hands with those who ventured to make organized religion free from bondage. To him it was a bondage of powers ever so satanic though as yet unrecognized by those in authority in Berlin and the East.

CHAPTER FIVE

Watchman in the Night

RONALD A. KNOX, Catholic Bible translator, son of a popular Anglican bishop, has ably remarked that Europe's disintegration was older and even more satanic than the deplorable atrophy which was to ruin the continent at a time when younger peoples all around the earth were rapidly rising to unprecedented power.

With its substitute religion of blood and race, nationalism could play the deuce after the French Revolution had divorced the raw material of human nature from the redeeming power of God's hallowing word. There was of course little cultural uplifting for the underdeveloped peoples in that neo-pagan era. Nor did the person, God's chosen instrument on the inhabited earth, count very much in a world bent upon self-glorification. Tacticians and experts in legality monopolized diplomatic relations. To that rule, neither the countries in possession of "hierarchies" nor those which had Protestant churches "established by law" were any notable exceptions. The impact of Christian ethics on international law and order was in decline throughout the era of Europe's enlightenment and emancipation. In the century following the triumph of the guillotine, any experiment in corporate life seemed permitted except where

27

it would imply a human being's responsibility under a living personal God.

What was left of the ancient and noble venture to decide international issues by person-to-person encounters was in danger of falling to pieces wherever the traditional bond between a constitutional government and a devoted people was undercut. In some respects, the Europe of 1900 was a pandemonium of sounds and reverberations. Only one voice was confined to a strictly private sphere: the voice of Christ and his church was not supposed to transcend the parochial line nor, in fact, to influence any channel of public relations.

It was, therefore, no wonder that church relations between the nineteenth century's great empires, Britain and Germany, did not develop in a way that would reveal a sense of truly Christian compulsion. Between the Church of England and the Protestants of Germany the major object of late nineteenth century disagreement was the very land where Jesus Christ became man, was brought to death, and rose again. Any state church system is apt to let sacred enterprises degenerate into issues of political prestige and diplomatic honor. In an era called liberal, old Germany's ecclesiastical statesmen felt unduly offended by the conventional terms on which some Anglican bishops separated all German elements, clerical, missionary, and educational, from ecumenical activities in the Holy Land.

Until finally Protestants of the non-established churches were to find a new international center in what was later known as the Augusta Victoria Foundation on the Mount of Olives, German indignation was bitter and deep. Had not both Britain's Queen Victoria and the last of Prussia's Frederick Williams set their seal on an agreement "to safeguard for ever" the Jerusalem bishopric as a joint undertaking with a view to a further coordination of Anglican and Lutheran orders and to occasional intercelebrations of the Holy Eucharist? That project was 60 years of age now, and nothing had come of it.

If in the nineteenth century some Anglican leaders were rather state- and empire-minded, the same was true of the liaison officers in old Germany's regional denominations. The office of a bishop smelled of Romanism and was therefore unacceptable to the state-supported advocates of liberal Protestantism. To speak of apostolic succession, moreover, was like questioning the continuity and authority of the Empire. You could be a liberal and even an agnostic as a state-church official, but you were not supposed to develop any sense of church-consciousness or any call to independent witness. Church loyalty had become a matter just as "private" and trivial as religion was and ever will be with socialist doctrinaires.

It was only after the "agnostic Edwardian interlude" that a new British king, George V, and a new archbishop, Randall Davidson, sincerely tried to inaugurate an era of renewed relations with the churches in central Europe. At that time the German authorities did not hesitate to respond to the well-meant Anglican move by helping to found an Alliance for Fostering Friendship Between the British and German Empires and Churches.

When, in the summer of 1912, a delegation was formed to pay a courtesy visit to Lambeth Palace and the London Court of St. James, no one thought it fitting to include Dibelius, although he could have served as a reliable interpreter wherever they went in Britain. He moved in circles where English was spoken with fluency. But then he kept standing too much aloof from the Prussian Court. Abandoning the time-honored life of vested interest and social prestige, he was no common adulator in government circles. He had been in Scotland for an unusual length of vacation, everyone knew this. But was not the Scottish mind rather unconventional and almost American in its "dour" and universal outreach?

No, young Dibelius had still to stay for a long period in Eastern Pomerania. When he was finally called to preach and help in the capital, there was little time left for saving or transforming organically the ancient Berlin tradition. He noted this not without some real dismay.

The spirit which all the Allies, now in warfare, rightly criticized was a spirit of overweening pride. The truth is that this spirit was not a legitimate outgrowth of what the Dibelius brothers cherished as the best of East Germany's traditions, the inheritance of the knights in holy orders who had left behind the safety and splendor of the Roman West, putting their hands to the plough to prove their fitness for the kingdom of God, his kingdom on the islands of the Baltic, on the plains of Prussia, and in all the virgin land of the east. Surely those primitive and dangerous areas were not to remain outside the field of that Sower who went forth to sow and remained patient even when his enemy came and sowed tares among the wheat and went his way.

The prewar signalizing of the coming reality (later to be called the ecumenical reality) already had its impact. The very lowliness of its first unfolding made the wartime preacher of Berlin's Church of the Holy Fount clearly stand out from state and empire frustration. When, in the cold November days of 1917, the heir to the Byzantine theocracy of premedieval times was shot by officers of an army mobilized to advance the cause of world revolution; and when, in the equally dark November days of 1918, the successor of the holy emperors ranging from Constantine the Great was dethroned by his own disorganized army, the peoples of Central and Eastern Europe were taken by horror and surprise. They wondered if jointly with sixteen-centuries-old traditions of law and order, the Protestant and Orthodox Churches would also fall to pieces in order to make way for monsters waiting now to establish the more worldly legacies of Byzantium and Rome. In Moscow there was for a prolonged time no positive answer to the awe-stricken people. In Berlin, however, there was.

Those who heard Dibelius preach on the Sunday after the first Armistice Day, were overwhelmed by his unerring instinct in evaluating the undercurrent of trends and movements likely to provide this century's consummation. The word on which he preached that Sunday after Germany's "inglorious revolution" came from Peter, first of Christ's apostles: "Be sober, be vigilant; because your adversary the devil, as a roaring lion, walks about, seeking whom he may devour."

Darkness and despair were the reward of a four-years' struggle which the German people had been taught to endure with dutiful patience. An order of life reaching back to Constantine's memorable decree of 313 A.D. and containing the tradition of a "commonwealth sacred to God's will with outlines for all the inhabited earth," was wiped out in a war which many hoped would make the world safe for democracy.

Democracy, it was true, had always been a foreign word to the average German. Partnership in the holding of political power had never been fought for with success. The burden of decision had seldom if ever fallen on the mass of the people. Even in religious affairs, the presentation of life's values and the bettering of society had been left to specific departments of the state-machinery.

After four years of sacrifice in warfare, the victorious spokesmen of democracy compelled the vanquished to sign a "quite voluntary declaration" that the whole German nation and no other entity of the world, bore the guilt of the bitterly lost war. The declaration went on to say that all reparation duties which the enlightened democrats imposed on the German people had to be accepted as a moral punishment for their own crime.

A messianic teaching of democracy, enshrined in such quasi-religious charters as the Covenant of the League of Nations, engendered in Germany words of self-annihilation which sounded quite pathetic, but which were even on the side of the German Marxists by no means sincere. These Socialists of the Marxist school who had waited for the breakdown of the imperial tradition with a devilish instinct of expectancy, were now very willing to harp on Germany's "militaristic perversion," besmirching every single trait that might otherwise have been thinkable as a starting point for reaffirming the nobler elements of German history.

To the Marxist doctrinaire it was of little interest how low the standard of morals of a new German generation was becoming. The Marxist pattern would stand out all the better for the chaos surrounding. Had it not been anticipated by Karl Marx, and was it not clearly proclaimed in Lenin's recent writings, that the monolith of western democracy was destined to crumble after another world war, as the Czars' and the Kaisers' realms had fallen overnight?

What then was to be expected from a Germany which tried democratic ways of self-administration and forms of government free from dynastic prerogatives for the first time? The rising generation, mostly fatherless as a consequence of war, were driven into a mood of such unrelieved uselessness that their outlet was either vice or crime or both. In the three years following the war the acts of violence, due to alcoholic excesses, rose from the stated average of 400 per year in Berlin to almost 3300. In Hamburg alone, treated cases of venereal diseases rose in 1924 by almost 300 per cent over against the average of the three previous years. The new government, composed as it largely was of Marxists including their milder shades and some Catholics, was too much of a farce to deal with these national depravities in any constructive way. In their failure to pay proper attention to the subtle workings of satanic powers throughout man's history, the dialectic and "progressive" types of the Marxist progeny were lighthearted enough to rest assured on the "intrinsic goodness of democratic man."

It was the Socialists in Central and Western Germany who proclaimed with all the finality and precision of profane philosophers that the Moscovite type of socialism, which of course they could not fully ignore, was not designed for expansion. In an essay one of the modern German "scientists" said: "The system in which the human individual counts only as the most advanced of earth's organic beings, the mammals of a gradual evolution, cannot and will not grow beyond the borderlines of the Slav and Mongolian tribes."

"Progressive" Socialists uttered forecasts like this: "A young generation of hopeful Germans whose search for pleasure is only too understandable should not be intimidated or even impressed by those inexorable Christian churches, as if it were feasible that a progressive German government would ever restrict pastors and priests in their ministries or individual liberties. Nor are such violating acts as witnessed inside Russia, such lowbred disregard of property and lives, thinkable in the Prot-

estant provinces of Germany, in the Oderland, Silesia, and
Pomerania."

During that formative period of a new Germany, the Roman
Catholic Church did not tackle the danger-potential inherent
in the Marxist philosophy. The minds of some prominent Catholics were still preoccupied by ecclesiastical rivalry. Anti-Prot-
estantism was in full swing. No wonder that the secular newcomers sensed the hour had come to persuade western Rhine-
landers and Bavarians that the "neutral" regime of the left was
far from disappointing. These opportunists said that the new
regime would deal with the nineteenth century alliance of
Protestantism and East German patriotism in full accordance
with the ideas of the modern rules of democracy, and with a
more final touch than the Catholics could ever apply.

The fruit thus reaped was bitter and poisoned. Every element of tradition, ranging from the hallowed belief in the European task assigned to the nation situated between East and
West, to the respect of property, insurance, endowments, and
legal grants, was ridiculed.

The pioneers of the Christian mission in the east, the valiant
knights of late medieval times, the founders of Protestant communities such as the Great Elector and the father of Frederick
II, and even Martin Luther, were derided by an "advance group"
of enlightened authors to whom cultural "advisers" in the allied camps lent ready ears. One of these advanced writers was
the first to go to Paris for a "peace reception" by the Sorbonne.
There he was said to have declared that Martin Luther's break
with the Roman Church was to some extent the outcome of a
spasmodic state of the brain peculiar to deformed species of
some eastern race and resulting in the most unpredictable vag-
aries. There was no end of charges against the greatest of the
Reformers to prove that his pride and temper had deformed the
Protestant majority of Germany until they evoked God's judgment, carried out by the nations of the West by way of depriving
the Germans of their disputed national identity.

At this time of utter impotence, Otto Dibelius looked around
for individual Christian witnesses in the western world who

might at last understand the resentment prevalent among the Protestants of Central Germany. East Germany, the area with the largest Protestant percentage, had already been cut asunder by the big Polish corridor, while Danzig, his first city parish, had been turned into what was labeled a "free state."

Dibelius was not slow to realize that it would be only a small minority of some Scottish Presbyterians in the British Commonwealth, and possibly some American Lutherans of German or Scandinavian descent, who might resist the poisoning influence in all the bargaining over German affairs. The vast majority of nominal Christians would be only too proud to mock at "Protestant Prussia." The "progressives" would continue for an undue period to shake their heads at the German want of adaptability, since the interpretation of God's will as it was cherished in Luther's heritage seemed to them so drastically inferior to all other systems of thought.

"Why don't the Lutherans of Saxony and Brandenburg readily admit that theirs has never been a church in the full sense which at least requires a well-ordered episcopate with a tradition older than that of the Reformation?" That was the question raised by one Anglican of fairly high standing. From those who associated with the episcopal office not only the well-being but the very essence of the church, came more and more regrets for the Lutheran and United Protestant Churches in Central Europe. Sincere though these regrets may have been, they were, in practice, quite useless.

The question which Dibelius asked was this: What is the scriptural justification for so many western churchmen's claims to finality and infallability? Why do they place their hope in a regeneration of Europe through the secular agents of democracy? To some agnostic French officials Dibelius wrote in 1920:

No church organization can claim to be perfect in the divine sense. At the same time, no church-conscious generation will betray the testimony given by its fathers in faith, without killing its very soul.

A church which changes its message with the change of governments is no church at all. Nor can the church be different *in peace from what it has been in wartime. We are not so sad about our Protestant church, despised though it may be by the mighty at present. We are much rather worried about the modern state; it pretends to be neutral and spiritually independent but is, in truth, the slave of selfish materialists, however nice and fashionable it may make itself appear.*

Such an assertion was firm and reassuring. People had begun to wonder what kind of authority, what degree of responsibility would be exercised by a church stripped of its imperial splendor and not fortified by a theory of bishops graced by apostolic succession. Was this, after all, the predicted time of thunderstorms to clear the air for a bright morning's vision of the city "whose chartered freemen are the true and the faithful?"

The church, still working in the dark of the night, was in truth more than just a historic order. It was, for one, the community of the people who had been to Wittenberg in their early days. It was also the fellowship of those who preferred poverty and outward misery in Berlin's still Protestant surroundings to the new Polish and Roman Catholic rule of Dibelius' own Danzig and the upper Oderland where his second son performed his pastoral work undauntedly. It was a firm and upright minority, ready to witness and ready to stand.

The day did come when men of another minority church, far beyond the Atlantic Ocean, saw the way clear for reassessment and reconciliation. On August 20, 1921 John Baltzer and Louis W. Goebel wrote to Old Prussia's church council that the Evangelical Synod of North America would be happy to have Otto Dibelius speak as a fraternal visitor at their General Conference to be held in New Bremen, Ohio, from September 28 to October 2 in the same year.

A long night was over. There were waiting in a boat beneath the Statue of Liberty, one mid-September morning, Louis W. Goebel and other "chartered freemen" of the coming church to whom the Christ-given office of reconciliation was not to be hidden throughout this century. They were waiting now to see the man who had watched over Europe when the night was dark and no light shining.

CHAPTER SIX

Old World Resurgent

THOSE WHO joined the Evangelical Synod leader to greet the man coming out of Germany's terrific thunderstorm were William F. McDowell, Methodist bishop in Washington, Arthur J. Brown of the Presbyterian Church, F. H. Knubel of the United Lutherans, and Charles S. Macfarland representing both the Federal Council and the Church Peace Union. Their meeting with Protestant Germany's first official postwar visitor was a real venture started out of a sense of Christian compulsion in the land of liberty.

To the man of Luther's heritage, the major meaning of liberty was the granting of a person's right to do his own thinking and to move about independent from another's tutelage. Such an independence which he had ever longed for included the free development of each county and state with none striving to dominate at the cost of the other. All noble features of such freedom, long precluded from the parceled and divided continent of Europe, he found happily fulfilled when he was taken from the imposing structure of New York City to travel via Pennsylvania and West Virginia to the more modest centers of the Evangelical Synod in Ohio. That pilgrimage through free and open stretches of country led him to a rethinking of the methods of congregational life and work in his homeland.

The Conference of New Bremen was the meeting which passed a resolution that a closer contact with the churches of a more Anglo-Saxon character should in the future be sought by the Synod. Public opinion was still rather anti-German in 1921. The change of climate which Dibelius' visit brought about in the fall of that year was based on the fact that he refrained from dwelling on any nostalgic patriotism. The principle, however, to which he held fast was that of mercy and reconciliation with the frustrated and the vanquished. No long speech was delivered by him. Yet the way in which he witnessed to Protestant Europe's appreciation of reopened contacts encouraged the *Evangelical Herald*, the Synod's monthly organ, to comment on Dr. Macfarland's over-enthusiastic appraisal of the Geneva spirit of that day:

The Church of Christ shall act as the conscience of all nations. She shall make provisions for truth having a proper place in international relations. She shall tolerate neither the suppression nor the distortion of facts. She shall resist all tendencies of spreading lies among the nations.

For the year 1921, those were bold words. The days of mockery at "the ever-lamenting Protestant minorities of Central Europe" had begun. In the years to follow, however, it became apparent that neither Roman Catholics nor the secular Marxists were able to retain the confidence of leading international diplomats. When the unstable government of the young Republic of Germany was given the opportunity to help open the way to a possible admittance to the League of Nations, the lack of decision appalled the whole of Europe.

To the surprise of the mocking peace-mongers who never missed a chance of ridiculing the "Protestants' nostalgia for their eastern domains," Dibelius came forward with his clear argument for Germany's true place in the European community. He did not join in the shallow applause of the League's accomplishments, over-advertised as they were already. Nor did he give his blessing to a pacifism combined with easygoing assent

to the *status quo*. Yet he advocated Germany's participation in
the League's work just as strongly as did his brother who had
expressed his positive views on the European outlook in the
preface to his two-volume book on Britain the year before.[1] In
stating the position of a new Germany in a new Europe, both
of them followed the suggestion of that profound thinker and
eloquent statesman Edmund Burke, who had said with his Irish
forthrightness, "It is the birthright privilege of freedom-seeking
Christians in all nations to transform the order of life by turning antagonists into partners."

Otto Dibelius' concise and surprising book on *The Church
and the League of Nations* made it clear to the world that in
Central Europe the church was coming into its own. The man
who had proceeded from an eastern minority to contact a less
despised, but equally devout and intercessive minority across the
Atlantic, brought something fresh and new into the history
of modern Europe. Incarnation was once more given to the
divine initiative in retracing a wholesome design for the most
war-stricken of all continents.

This design was indeed the coming great embodiment of
what a humble Christian at an almost forgotten prewar gathering of intercontinental pioneers had called the only essential
and life-saving reality of the twentieth century. Though the herald of that prophetic judgment, William Temple, was not destined to live until the end of the century's second war, there
was long to survive a fellow pilgrim who could not ignore and
would not abandon the common vocation recognized by Europeans, Americans, and Australians at the dawn of this century. So it was given to Temple's contemporary to proclaim
that in the ongoing century, no European nation could lead
a life purely for its own perpetuation without creating new disorder and harm in the international sphere.

The decidedly non-Christian diplomats who remodeled Eu-

------

[1] A posthumous English edition of William Dibelius' *England* was
published by J. Cape and Harrison Smith, London, Toronto, and New
York in 1934.

rope after the first war imposed their nationalistic conceptions on the many states that were the result of Central Europe's disintegration. Into the small units which had seldom or never complained of the infringement of their cultural identities, diplomats instilled a far too patriotic pride. Failing to evaluate the world's deeper trend which pointed toward integration of greater political and geographical units, the unimaginative Versailles and Geneva experts deemed it appropriate to add national churches to each of the new small states. As if such plans were not fanciful enough, the national churches had to adopt a narrow sectarian outlook. In countries like Poland and Lithuania there were ecclesiastical statesmen who showed a regrettable readiness to support the fateful attempts at making the churches into abodes of graven images representing monstrous ideas blended with some semi-Christian elements.

With an obscure kind of continuity, the continent was once more pursuing the way of self-seclusion and deterioration. The French nation, victorious and self-assertive as it was at the time, seemed not too unhappy that the United States of America were absorbed by their own affairs. No leading churchman of France had been to the States as Otto Dibelius had.

It was once more the "eastern Protestant" who vividly recalled the scope and amplitude of American culture including American church life, when he tried to heed the invitations that reached him from those eastern people who thought he might be the man to redeem them from the strange impositions of the state philosophers and agnostics. He sat down to think how counsel and comfort could be brought to the faithful of Austria, Hungary, Czechoslovakia, Rumania, and the Baltic States. In all those states, left-wing socialism already occupied a position of power. When Dibelius came forward with a most illuminating research work under the challenging title, "State Frontiers No Barriers for the Church," French secular influence was so extensive that an English publication was not feasible. In the twenties, there was no William Temple residing in London's Lambeth Palace.

Some British churchmen were interested in extending inter-

communion and coordination of ecclesiastical offices with Orthodox churches of apostolic succession. But the suffering of the
faithful in the early years of the Soviet Union was never made
the subject of an official church protest. Nor did anyone in
Geneva voice criticism when the Communists began to under-
mine the Orthodox church institutions in Bulgaria. Dibelius
published some of the pathetic letters received from Bishop
Irenaeus of Novi Sad and Professor Zankov of Sofia. No one
in Western Europe seemed to pay attention to the atrocious
balkanization of Southeast Europe. The only slogan in which
the accredited diplomats of Geneva seemed interested was, No
more war.

To some the slogan No more war seemed like a godsend. In
reality it was an imperative that took away the ancient freedom of choice with regard to the highest things in human history. A negative slogan relieved the European of taking any
risk, of strengthening the power to challenge, of actively choos-
ing between the lesser of two given evils. No wonder that
America withdrew the greater part of its sponsorship from the
Geneva institution. The blunting of the moral sense, the lack
of spiritual insight, and the tacit acceptance of evil seemed incompatible with America's concept of world stewardship.

Some honestly devout churchmen sought refuge in the fervent expectation of global destruction, the end of all organic
life. "This is earth's last century. The Bible has it that none
of us shall survive the year 2000," was a saying often heard
from pious individuals in the twenties. Dibelius thought that
even in the short span of some seventy years it was worth while
to take up the gauntlet thrown down by the deniers of Christ.
If his century was to have such a paramount place in the sum-
ming up of mankind's history, he would like to have it labeled
not the age of murder and fornication, but rather the century
in which the Church of God had come into her own, her
tears wiped away from her eyes, her body restored in purity
and serene deliverance from the kings of this earth.

In that first postwar period, when the term *kingdom* was
still a very institutional one, largely used by Europe's conserva-

tive historians without any scriptural comprehension, Dibelius reminded the whole of Europe that the real pledge of the church was not to restore earthly kingdoms but to proclaim the sovereignty of Christ the King. The ultimate reign of Christ would never be confined to the private sphere of some saved individuals:

Individual belief, emotional as it tends to be, is ever so liable to disregard the things pertaining to the kingdom of God. The kingdom-element of life under God has often been left to the powers that be and has become sadly disjointed.

A continent torn asunder by war may need a great revival of faith if it is to become part of the kingdom, power field and dynamic requisite of a church united in service and action. The horrible war which lies behind us has certainly not engendered a religious revival. On the contrary, a fear of the future, a sense of uncertainty and utter insecurity have come to fill the hearts of many Europeans.

That good Samaritan, the leader of the Swedish church, speaks of an ecumenical revival. I wish such a revival were happening in the heart of Germany. However, we cannot compel it. If such a revival does not come overnight, that is no reason to blow up in hysterics. On the other hand, the absence of a natural drive in evangelism does not mean that we should remain passive altogether.

Europe's churches may have been unworthy of its great treasure in the last century. It remains a global fact, however, that the movement for Christ is still in the ascendant. Let us only find out the direction in which the word of God is advancing. Let us explore where the strongest response is given to the word. Let us examine the soil where it has taken roots in order to show to all mankind a new order of the ages.

Of all Europeans, those endowed with a traditional training in theology were the most reluctant to recognize that America incorporated a spirit and a venture of its own. All the traditional textbooks of the continent had it that the civilization of the United States was an outsized and largely misshaped extension of the culture and glory that was Europe. "Outsized" meant skyscrapers, or the equally limitless schemes of developing resources of forest, field, and mine. For a long time, leading Europeans would continue to regard America's "exaggerated language" out of character and her towering scale utterly failing to reveal the deepest secrets of God.[2]

It has been said that the greater part if not all of the criticism which Otto Dibelius had to encounter in the years to follow was due to his untraditional and "strangely positive appraisal of the new world." His original and very human sense of historical places and persons had made him eager at an early time to catch the excitement of the American experience in the fulfilment of an almost superhuman task set there by nature and history alike. The glorious optimism of John R. Mott, the first of modern Christian laymen, was still a potent force with him, as unforgettable as Edinburgh's prewar gathering of the coming great church.

If Edinburgh and the glory that was Scotland had still a historical meaning, then it might be that the "new order of the ages" was not a monopoly of the American nation in whose Great Seal it was imprinted and engraven. The finest of all pledges ever formulated by American leaders, was re-echoed in Dibelius' heart and will whenever opportunities of the old world failed to provide Europe's rising generation with a program for reconstructive action: ". . . with firmness in the right, as God gives us to see the right, let us strive on to finish the work we are in . . . to do all which may achieve and cherish a just and lasting peace. . . . "[3] Not that the heir of East Germany's knights in order would ever wish to leave his native soil and become an American by naturalization. He deemed it a greater call to strengthen the intercontinental partnership by reinforcing the sobering effect of America's mounting responsibility in a rapidly changing and narrowing world.

---

[2] Geoffrey Fisher, Archbishop of Canterbury, "The Americans and Ourselves," in *The Christian News-Letter*, London, January 1955; reprinted in *Christianity and Crisis*, vol. 15, no. 7, pp. 49 ff.

[3] From Abraham Lincoln's second inaugural address, March 4, 1865.

When in 1925 Otto Dibelius passed on the Orthodox Bishop of Novi Sad's pathetic report on the dynamite plot in Sofia Cathedral aimed at the Bulgarian king, but actually killing some twenty worshipers and wounding many more, the most helpful expression of sympathy and relief came from the American churches he had visited in 1921. While the softheaded and irresponsible among European diplomats still deplored the United States' withdrawal from the Geneva platform, Dibelius pointed out with deep satisfaction that the truest and best of American forces had come into the scene of Europe through interchurch aid, a Christian policy of sharing and giving.

It was in the middle of the twenties that he began to read regularly American journals of history, literature, and law. He took decisions of the United States Supreme Court seriously and counted how often they began with the statement, "We are a Christian people." When European loyalists of traditional standing prophesied that all governmental authority was doomed to perish after the forceful dethroning of crowned monarchs, Dibelius would point out that a president's oath of office on the open Bible was hardly less an act of responsible stewardship than any noble king's coronation by the anointed hands of an archbishop.

In evaluating the Christian background of the American mission and venture, he found little acclamation in the Europe of the twenties. It was an accepted saying that the States had entered the first great war in order to make the world safe for democracy. Very few, however, would acknowledge that democracy implies partial surrender and an adjustment not only on the national, but also on the personal scale. The virtues of adjustment and surrender, basically founded on the will to sacrifice something for the neighbor and the brother, were not readily given their proper place in the European order of values. The act of personal surrender was particularly foreign to the theology of state religion. The deity of the state was strong and rigid with particular demands on the subjects. The one approach in which the statist archpriests were not interested, was the person-to-person relation. And it was just this rigidly cold and impersonal type of quasi-religion which the man of Wittenberg, after his return from the new world, was anxious to have eliminated forever.

Before he appealed to some church leaders outside Germany to grapple with the task of Europe's reconstruction he wrote these words of avowal and self-consolation:

They say I am not a good German in the traditional sense, because I spoke of a freeing thunderstorm after the downfall of an empire which they called holy. God knows I never cared for violent defeats or losses or wounds. I only felt it was God's will to make the Protestant Church independent from state control.

They say my American journey was no good because I did not bring home with me support for an authoritarian state which some of my seniors are eager to re-establish complete with unity of throne and altar. What a fulsome sight, what a limited horizon over many of our ecclesiastical institutions! How defacing and discomforting this autumnal tang of lament for the ages long ago!

Don't they realize that with the increase of world-wide communication the nations are growing nearer one toward the other? Should they not gladly follow the vision of a church that takes advantage of wider mutual contact, mutual experience, and mutual concern? What joy and comfort can they derive from immolating their souls on the altar of a monolith?

The perilous idea of a church adorning the authoritarian state by presenting a show of numbers, producing prominent statistics, and gloating over some functional efficiency, has no place with the spirit of the new day.

In some distant corners of our rapidly changing and narrowing world, I can see the rays of a real morning. While I go on working in the dark, I will not be discouraged. True light sends out its first rays with ever so faint and tender illumination. But these tender rays have all the morrow's virgin purity, the holy angel's brightness, her promise of delivery from despondency and darkness, and on that promise rests my fondest hope, to see the acceptable hour.

CHAPTER SEVEN

Facing the Challenge

THE PASTOR of Berlin's Church of the Holy Fount
set out to appeal in person to leaders of the European churches
for the continent's reconstruction along the lines of the Christian message, along the lines of solidarity, of healing and forgiveness. Such plans were not being formulated in the atmosphere of Geneva. But among traditional churchmen also Dibelius encountered coldness of heart and formal reserve. It is
only fair to remember the few great men who appeared per-
sonable and approachable where most continental leaders shut
their hallowed doors to "the man who never seems to outgrow
his youthful enthusiasm," or, to quote a more pointed libel,
"the prototype of intercontinental confusion."

Foremost among the fine Europeans who did not sneer but
listened and encouraged, was Albert Schweitzer. In the same
sad twenties which saw the old world resurgent, he came to
Berlin to secure support and intercession for the noble and sacred enterprise of Lambaréné. Before he addressed a public
audience, he went to Holy Fount parsonage. So impressed was
he with the pastor's study on the process of dechristianization
in Central and East Germany, that he quietly changed the second part of the evening's program. He drew an unexpected

parallel between the French mission to Western Africa and Berlin's mounting responsibility for the east of Europe. He said every Christian was called to be a partner in missions throughout this century:

I can see you have a tremendous work before you in the eastern parts of Martin Luther's land and even in this great city, beleaguered as it is by infernal forces, the spirits of darkness which I have seen from another angle of the earth. You have heard of our great pledge in the heart of Africa. I feel you are willing to give some little contribution to the pledge, to the glory of the Prince of Light. Tonight, your offering will be accepted by myself for the Protestant relief and welfare mission in Berlin, in Potsdam, and in Berlin's eastern surroundings.

Dibelius, who was present, protested against this turning of the tide, but Schweitzer's will prevailed. The night's offering was tremendous in size. What was even more meaningful, it represented an honest and deep commitment of souls inspired and united in an enterprise of light and regeneration which knew no barriers.

The second churchman who received Dibelius with a warm and loving heart was Irenaeus, Orthodox Bishop of Novi Sad in Yugoslavia. He was glad to join with Dibelius in setting up the welfare teams of the Gustavus Adolphus Foundation giving honor to the Swedish king who gave his life to save continental Protestantism from the atrocities of the Counter-Reformation. Through this cooperative effort relief was brought to the thousands of Protestants scattered all over Slovenia and Croatia after the breaking up of the Austro-Hungarian empire, and to those in Czechoslovakia and the Baltic.

The third good Christian who appreciated Dibelius' efforts was a Danish bishop in a former German province. He was Valdemar Ammundsen, chairman of the World Alliance for International Friendship. Dibelius admired Ammundsen's impartial handling of the new German frontier situation. He was even more deeply moved by Ammundsen's response to his plea

fotografia

Otto Dibelius with Bishop of Leitmeric in Czechoslovakia;
during Lent 1955

Otto Dibelius with Sergej J. Stragorodskij, Patriarch of Moscow,
and the Bishop of Greifswald, Pomerania; 1949

dpa-Bild

Above, after opening of British Parliament by Queen, London, 1955, with assistant, Foreign Relations Office

Left, at New Bremen, Ohio, September 1921 with John Baltzer, President of Evangelical Synod of North America, and Dibelius' assistant for Minorities Relief Work in Halle, East Germany for the Protestant minorities in the provinces ceded to Catholic Poland under the Treaty of Versailles. In opposition to the Polish advocate of a state-connected Lutheran Church, Dibelius and Ammundsen persuaded the Minorities Committee of the World Alliance to issue a strong statement in Geneva which drew the attention of the League of Nations to Poland's outmoded nationalism. The secret of this successful document lay in its rethinking and restating of the whole Christian position in the modern world. In full agreement, Dibelius and Ammundsen proclaimed that the Christian community is bound to be a minority:

The dream of clerical rule is a thing of the past. The churches united in the World Alliance for International Friendship are minority units throughout the continent. They do not claim to govern the whole of their nations. But they desire to have the fundamental rights of worship in their respective mother tongues, also the rights of assembling and publishing safeguarded to them as loyal members of a church which is basically a universal church.

Danish patriotism had been frightfully anti-German for almost a century. Dibelius knew the reason for that only too well. It seemed a miracle that churchmen of totally different national outlooks should act in a joint protest against the authoritarian outlawing of minorities living in Poland and the Baltic States.

With regard to the Baltic States, Dibelius' great plan was to make the German and Scandinavian churches instrumental in operating a Protestant faculty independent from state control, either in Latvia or in Lithuania. He never tired of visiting the struggling Protestant communities in both countries. In the mud and dirt of Lithuania, he was often advised to travel overnight. During the daytime, supervision and spying already appeared to function all too well in a country where the majority had in turn become used to Russian and Roman methods of inquisition. In the Baltic area, Dibelius had for the first time to cope with the sad performances of two totalitarian systems.

In his eastern campaign for safeguarding rightful minority claims, he found two more allies in the Norwegian Lutheran Church. They were Jens Gleditsch, Bishop of Nidaros, and John Tandberg, Bishop of Oslo. They did a good work in breaking down the wall of scorn and insensibility concerning any ideas or plans beyond the grasp of statist diplomacy. Tandberg was bold enough to label the first world war as "the natural child of the French Revolution." Without the brotherly support from Scandinavia, even the most active of German pastors could not have enabled the sadly harassed church of Lithuania to acquire corporation status for that Protestant faculty which was to train the clergy for Protestant churches in all the Baltic states.

In his holy commitment to a Christ-inspired reconstruction of the continent, Dibelius' greatest ally and possibly the greatest friend in his whole life was Sweden's Nathan Söderblom. He was fourteen years older than Dibelius, and his extensive traveling experience was unique. For several years he had done pastoral work in Paris, and academic work in Leipzig.

Söderblom's American experience dated back to Mount Hermon, Northfield, Connecticut. There in 1890, the lay evangelist Dwight L. Moody and the student volunteer John R. Mott had greeted young Nathan with fervent prayers and sent him back with a great vision:

Not only for Scandinavia, but for the whole of Europe there shall be formed a uniting bond of solidarity and service, so that the saved disciples, the earnest followers of Christ, need no longer depend on the state-connected churches.

It took thirty-five years of rising states and empires, devastating wars and breath-taking revolutions to realize the essential parts of the Northfield vision.

The blatant era of secularism was still in full swing, and the year was 1925. Nathan Söderblom, raised to the ancient archbishopric of Upsala, sent out invitations under the heading of Oxenham's hymn, the words of farewell in Mott's and Moody's evensong:

Join hands then, brothers of the faith,
Whatever your race may be—
Who serves my Father as a son,
Is surely kin to me.

There came to Stockholm, Nathan Söderblom's and Gustavus Adolphus' Swedish capital, in the summer of 1925 not only French, Swiss, Dutch, and British Protestants, but also the vastly different representatives of America's big denominations. The remarkably heterogeneous company included the Egyptian Patriarch of Alexandria, the Bulgarian Metropolitan of Sofia, and the Yugoslav Archimandrite of Belgrade. Irenaeus and Zankov, Dibelius' allies, were also present. Without the inclusion of those Orthodox dignitaries, the new Christian Council for Life and Work would not have been entitled to assume the prefix *universal* which was so greatly congenial to Mott's and Moody's classic watchword—*to evangelize the world in our generation.*

Dibelius was deeply moved to have a reunion with some of the early leaders of the ecumenical movement to whom he had looked up when he was a junior visitor to the International Missionary Conference in Edinburgh, a quarter of a century earlier. One friend who was missing in Stockholm was William Temple, then Bishop of Manchester. But Arthur J. Brown of the great Presbyterian Church was as helpful to the German Lutheran as he had been in New York four years before. The heart and soul of the unprecedented gathering, the greatest of all Lutherans, was Sweden's Nathan Söderblom.

Though Söderblom had received his frame of mind and outlook largely in the nineteenth, most utopian of all centuries, he was too modest in nature to indulge in any super-church perfectionism. His true example was a man of the sixteenth, most religious of all centuries, Gustavus Adolphus. It was he who had saved continental Protestantism by his militant martyrdom. With his deep sense of coming events, with his truly inspired imagination, Archbishop Nathan Söderblom could see that a new martyrdom was part of the unquestionable design of the divine Judge to whom high and low are subjects.

Of all governments in the world, only one had prevented those churchmen living within its domains from attending the first World Assembly in Stockholm. Söderblom wondered whether this might be a prelude to some attempt at eliminating the name of Jesus Christ also west of the Russian borderline. In that context, these were his words, spoken in 1926:

Not all of Europe will be lost to Christian religion and cul-ture. There is still the valiant Protestant element of Germany's eastern parts. And then there is the living soul of that fine and hopeful movement for all Germany's regeneration, Dr. Otto Dibelius.

The words did not become known to Dibelius until six years later. It was the archbishop's widow who reported them first. They were stated afresh by a man whom Söderblom had en-trusted with a relief mission to the Baltic, Dr. Oscar Schabert. This good Samaritan approached Dr. Dibelius to join him in a pilgrimage to the Latvian Martyrs' Stone, dedicated to those who had been killed by Soviet intruders in the city of Riga.

Violent world revolution was in the air. The challenge was directed not merely against organized religion or ecclesiastical titles, but against the very birthright of man to live up to his calling, to speak and to pray in his mother tongue, to center around himself what he rightly demands for all humanity. All this was being questioned in a more massive and, therefore, more obstructive way than in the era of ancient Rome.

The question of this century's revolution has to be faced still, and answered too. The first answer was contained in the most revolutionary book published between the two great wars in Europe, with the title *The Century of the Church* (1927):

The net is closing around us. The churches of Christ are en-tering a new era. New ventures emerge. New responsibilities confront us all. Amidst the pandemonium of shrill voices of hatred, there rings through a clear call for true Christian broth-erhood, sometimes still very faint, but then also never heard before with such a fervent kind of crescendo.

People may like to pass all sorts of verdicts about their parishes and denominations, yet there can be no doubt that this will be called the century of the coming great church.

The hour is nearing when the Protestants of Central Europe will awaken to find themselves vital elements of a world-wide movement. Forces whose roots are the most deeply implanted of the West will be seen holding up and on high the church renewed for all the inhabited earth.

Where, then, is the generation ready to give to the newcoming church an impact both human and holy?

What a creditable undertaking, to swim against the violent current! What a praiseworthy pledge, to hold the banner high in spite of the firing at the faithful few by the encircling foes.

Here is the chance to follow Christ in the simple way of bearing his cross, and to be committed to a cause for which the living God himself pleads ever so firmly as he safeguards the advance of his fellow-workers. The cause of the coming true church is a cause mightily furthered by that holy storm forecast by prophets within the covenant. The "diabolic and evil angels" are compelled to say "Aye" while the servants of light proclaim that the watching for the dawning of a brighter day is not in vain.

When those words were written, the battleground of Central Europe had still to prove its central position in that predicted global strife between the children of light and those of darkness.

CHAPTER EIGHT

Totalitarian Sunset

THE AUTHOR of *The Century of the Church* had spent his early and decisive years in those eastern areas desperately desired by various nations and then disputed as a bulwark against the West. Would he be deceived into aggressive action when Satan managed to present to the continent a magnetic person intent on thwarting the divine order of "joy in righteousness"?

It has been said that "if Hitler, the strangely magnetic and mentally diseased Austrian artist, had not risen to inflict doom and agony on countless millions, the great effort of Christian reconstruction in Eastern Europe might have succeeded."[1] Far too many came to cherish such evasive views on the devil's varied craftsmanship. However, the men who incorporated the Protestant conscience of a vastly estranged nation followed an independent, and narrow, way. Within a fellowship of the most conscientious commitment, Dibelius meditated on the historic meaning of God's early covenant. With his partners in that covenant, he sustained himself in prolonged prayer be-

---

[1] George N. Shuster, *Religion Behind the Iron Curtain*, p. 10. Macmillan, 1954.

fore taking up the gauntlet thrown down to all Christian people by the political leader who, with all his effrontery, presumed to take God's law into his own hands.

Like many a dictator, Hitler attempted to make the Church of Christ the great harlot of the world's mighty. As soon as he came to power, he, the lapsed Catholic, requested the former state church to send "an agreeable dignitary of Protestant lineage" to say a few words of "friendly greeting" before his solemn act of accession in the Kaiser's church at Potsdam. When the Protestant Board of Church Administration announced that they would send Dibelius, Hitler at once intimated it might be better to have a proper worship service in a different sanctuary even though he would offer his self-composed oath of allegiance to the spirit of the eternal Nordic race in the Kaiser's church.

The year was 1933. The Kaiser's old General and honest adviser, aged Reich President Von Hindenburg was still alive. He came to the place where Dibelius preached on the Day of Potsdam. That was the Church of St. Nicholas, less imperial in splendor and yet erected on the very site where just a thousand years earlier the blood of the first Christian martyrs had reddened the soil of eastern lands. What Dibelius now said on the site of the valiant martyrs' tomb was essentially different from the perfunctory word of salute which the fascist usurper had expected. Dibelius compared two scripture passages which revealed the two angles from which state and government attained their alternative meaning. The first text was Paul's saying that "there is no governing authority except from God. For rulers are not a terror to good conduct, but to bad" (Romans 13); the other text was John's vision of a rising state deity which was no longer "God's servant for your good." The new goddess of the earth was wilfully discarding apostolic sanction. These were the words Dibelius now read and interpreted in the light of contemporary history: "I saw a beast rising out of the sea, having seven heads and ten horns, and upon his horns ten crowns, and upon his heads a blasphemous name. And they worshiped the beast, saying, Who is like the beast, and who will fight against it?" (Revelation 13). He was firm and prophetic:

We do not resist authority, since to do so is anarchy and thus irreligious. But as soon as the state demands to be the church itself; as soon as the state enforces more than law-abiding from its subjects; as soon as the state strives to assume power to rule the souls of men—then we are asked by Luther's words to exercise resistance in the name of God.

When the Confessing Church, that first self-governing brotherhood of German ministers and lay people, arose against the Austrian usurper, Dibelius became a member of its leading body, the *Bruderrat* (Brethren's Council). He never exhausted his soul and mind with issues ably fabricated by the Hitler party out of failures and anomalies of the German state church of the past. It was, of course, unthinkable that he should conduct any public service. Under the first totalitarian authority it was only natural that on one midwinter morning early in 1934, the new State Church Commissar came round to Dibelius' office building, which was attached to his residence, to tell him that he had to move his furniture (apart from eight filing cabinets already confiscated) to a garage across the road within forty-eight hours. For his family there was a kitchen and three servants' rooms over that garage.

When Dibelius patiently settled down in that extraordinary abode, he realized that neither a continued conferring with his younger clergy nor any extension work was feasible in such dark squalor. So he thought about new ways of contacting the ministers who looked for his brotherly counsel. Many of them depended on his spiritual and personal help; they were the ministers who had not yielded to the Nazi idea that a sermon should always be ready for examination by cultural commissars on the Thursday previous to the Sunday on which it was to be preached. Those who agreed to that kind of censorship received complete sermons in uniform pattern before Saturday afternoon, so that in memorizing them they would harmonize their forms of thought and speech with the secular philosophy of the Nazi deity.

Those who did not conform also received stenciled sermons

and information sheets, but sometimes late on Saturday evening! These outlines were not brewed in the culture-mongers' caldron, but handwritten in the backroom over that Steglitz garage where through holy guidance a publicly despised ex-preacher reformulated what the true church would still have to say, no matter how broadly the gates of hell were opened.

Dibelius' three daughters and two young laymen, one of them a student in his brother's seminary, used to type and duplicate on Wednesdays what was written by hand earlier each week. On Thursdays, Dibelius set out for his nightly journeys through the vast area of Eastern Brandenburg. He had acquired a tiny car for the purpose and liked to drive it himself. His wife would accompany him only when the worship and information material was not so copious as to take up all the seating accommodation. By Saturday midnight there was hardly a single minister of the Confessing Church not equipped with the means of conveying the message of him who has risen to redeem those who wish to follow along the narrow way.

Those who saw the new chauffeur back on Sunday morning from his extensive expeditions, can never forget how miraculously his peace, a spirit of grace rather than of accomplishment, transformed his physical exhaustion into a deeply devotional attitude as he sat in a back pew of the nearby Dahlem parish church. But that parish of St. Anne was not to have peace, nor was any long time given Dibelius to serve as a traveling agent of the true church, now labeled an illegal and subversive organization.

At St. Anne's in Dahlem, the minister was the courageous naval ex-commander Martin Niemoeller. He had just returned from a short retreat with Dibelius at a western spa when he was arrested in his parsonage by Hitler's gestapo. Dibelius, forbidden to shepherd the orphaned congregation with the comfort of God's word from the pulpit, asked younger colleagues to hold daily services of intercession, which lasted over a period of nearly five years. He himself added Sundays to his travel programs in order to inform and to pledge the faithful of the more outlying parts of his former province.

There is full truth in Christ's saying that the children of darkness are, in their generation, wiser than the children of light. Engaged in his Christ-inspired attempts at clarifying the complex situation of the rising Nazi empire, Dibelius one day reached the ancient center of Ruppin County. One of the confessing pastors suggested that he should publicly make it clear to the misguided but harmless looking Nazis of that rural town that they were wrong in assuming that they could follow both Christ and Hitler.

Accepting the invitation, the pastor of pastors chose the eighth chapter of the Gospel according to John to make it tangible that in the life of everyone who wished to witness to God's truth, a moment would come when he had to choose between great loyalties. Christ had not wilfully abandoned the fine heritage of his House of David; yet he had to say to the Rome-supported Pharisees, "Ye are from beneath, I am from above. Ye are of this world. . . . " Dibelius read and expounded the context of the whole chapter. There was, however, a Judas-like clerical named Falkenberg who watched as Dibelius read. He was quick to instruct his brown-shirted entourage of peasants and coarse-voiced traders to await the oncoming assault, "Ye are from beneath." Readily they fell in with beery-voiced shouts of "Traitor and enemy of the people." Within three minutes the beer-garden hall resembled a battlefield strewn as it was with broken glasses, spilled bottles, and splintered chairs.

That drama of a late November week-end in the middle thirties of our century ended almost like the first-century drama of Stephen. If there were no stones among the objects cast at the traveling disciple, there was yet on the same night arrest and solitary confinement in the jail of that rural township.

What had Dibelius said in his youth some twenty years earlier, when Stoecker, the Thomas Chalmers of Berlin, was ostracized by Wilhelm, last of the Kaisers?

Real witnesses who give their life and liberty for the cause of Christian liberty—we have not had them here in Central Europe since long before the Reformation.

CHAPTER NINE

Never Off Duty

THE WATCHMAN set on the wall to guard the people of God was no longer doing his appointed work. There was no man of vision to warn the many who were accustomed to firm and inspired leadership. Now they heard only the voice of strangers.[1]

In the whole of Germany, the people of God had obviously forfeited their birthright. The prophet to whom the faithful had looked up as to a Nehemiah for the rebuilding of the beloved city was silenced behind the walls and bars of a prison. Those of his people who did not bow unto Baal, now went into hiding. Those who remained on the surface by taking part in public functions could do little to prevent the pagan intruders from identifying the cause of religion with the interests of the usurpers. But were they all nothing but *Christians by convenience?*

The silenced bearer of the cross was filled with shame and sorrow. The guards of his cell in Ruppin County Prison, and

---

[1] At this time, Karl Barth, the prophet among the Confessing Churchmen, was already back in his native Switzerland. For Dibelius' appraisal of Barth see Appendix.

the young gestapo officers who took him over to Potsdam for a thorough hearing, told him of some of his former colleagues who against their better judgment had expressed their loyalty to the Nazis. Theirs was a hypocritical expression of loyalty— even the gestapo officers were sure of that. But in a country where the dogma of justification by faith alone had been misconstrued to the extent of isolation and distortion, what did man's inward faith and conviction matter?

The prophets of the blood-and-race religion were fully satisfied by outward professions of loyalty and cooperation. Theirs was a dogma without the Spirit. To a people bereft of the Spirit, Christ himself was no longer a guide across the times, no longer a shepherd heard and envisaged to bring those other sheep which did not belong to his fold. This was the time of the hirelings. For a further period of ten years, the stage was set for a savage drama of blood, carnality, and murder.

No more criticism based on Christ-guided decisions. No more pronouncements evolving from concepts higher than the grossly materialistic dogmas of the state. No presentation of ultimate values, since even the historical order of the past was being cut down, rashly subordinated to the political expediency of the day.

So lamed and terrified were the passive and law-abiding people by the subtle joining of treason and pressure, that the man who really was responsible for that intrigue and provocation thought the time was ripe for him to come into the open and to apply still more drastic methods to the pastor of pastors. The man behind the scene was Hans Kerrl, Reich Minister for Religious Affairs.

After a conditional release to the top garage flat, Otto Dibelius was constantly guarded, while Kerrl summoned all party leaders charged with "cultural affairs" to his imposing state-church office. The fight against the revolutionary church resistance leaders was only in its beginning stage, the minister said. A committee was now created to perform the task of issuing outlines for Sunday sermons in keeping with the new religion of blood and race.

The first of these outlines for uniform preaching were formulated by Hans Kerrl himself:

*The concept of man's self-perfection shall henceforth replace
the old-fashioned doctrine of reconciliation with God the Father
through the Son.*

*To preach about such an illusory relation as that of Father,
Son, and Holy Spirit is contrary to the realities of the new
race-conscious human beings.*

To maintain the divinity of Christ is ridiculous.

*God's will is infiltrated and inscribed in the blood of the
Nordic race. Submission to such pre-Nordic and non-Teutonic
confessions as the Apostles' Creed is shallow and incompatible
with the racial standard of our people and its celestial blend of
blood and temper.*

Hundreds had been obliged to listen to these "First Outlines
for New Ways of Worship and Religious Action." Among those
listeners, 450 in all, there were some who became suddenly disillusioned. Changing their brown nazi uniforms for inconspicuous civilian dress, they asked Dibelius' daughters when
there were possible intervals in the day and night guard shifts.
Two of the disillusioned Nazis actually appeared at the back
yard of the garage in the dark of night. With seeming agitation, they declared they had for a long time been misguided.
A third one wrote a clandestine letter to Dibelius saying much
the same as the other two had confessed: Those outlines for
worship were more than they could really stand. They would
rather submit to Dibelius the words of Kerrl and the list of all
officials summoned to hear him announce the new church program. Might it not be that the man of Wittenberg, the unforgotten leader of the young, could do something about it? The
repentant Nazis felt sure the mass of Christian people would
still stand up in protest if only their rightful guide and shepherd
raised his accredited and truthful voice to comment on the new
drive on the church's doctrine and life.

Dibelius wondered how he, no longer permitted as a shepherd
to reach his own flock, could make a pronouncement without

acting against the law of the land. Preaching was forbidden to
him. The driving license and travel permit were withdrawn from
him after the provocative incident in rural Ruppin County.
However, there was one thing he would still risk in spite of the
Reich minister's warning to keep silent. He would write an
open letter to that minister, saying in substance: The Nazi
outlines for preaching were a source of disturbance to many
Christians in many lands. He thought he had better give Christian advice and a pastoral comment on what was now spreading
like wildfire. He considered it to be his solemn obligation to let
the creator of a new kind of worship and the peoples affected by
it realize what was at stake. After these introductory remarks,
Dibelius proceeded to write what the forgiveness of sins, the
reconciliation with his heavenly Father, and the spiritual presence of his divine brother, Christ the Son of the Father, had
meant in his own life.

It was an open letter, yet it was very personal. The mighty
leader to whom it was addressed was taken seriously as a person.
Any man, Dibelius knew, was a living instrument capable of
taking decisions in any direction, even the most unexpected:

*There is a glorious secret about each individual person. The
secret implies surprising changes, if only one personal challenge
comes from the outside, opening the heart and restoring the
Father's image.*

In the cosmic array of personal beings, there are the sinister
secrets too. The often disguised character of the Reich minister
was displayed when he read the unsealed letter for himself. He
became furious and frenzied. Very soon he set in motion the
whole mechanism of that Nazi procedure which was to destroy
twelve million people in twelve years' time.[2]

A show trial was carefully prepared and elaborately staged. In
Berlin's biggest law court, Kerrl appeared in a storm-trooper's
brown uniform, escorted by a host of brown comrade leaders
and some black bodyguards complete with death's-head cock-

---

[2] *Gestapo: Instrument of Tyranny*, Edward Crankshaw. Viking, 1956.

ades. Kerrl opened the proceedings by shouting at the High Attorney the accusation of "Otto Dibelius, a disfrocked clergyman":

"I accuse him of wilful lying against me, a minister of the German world power commissioned by the great Leader. I have never said that to believe in Jesus as the Son of God is ridiculous. Since the accused has written down this lie, I do not only indict him of a personal offence which would require only a sentence of imprisonment. I also accuse him of violating the regulation according to which he was ordered to stay in his home without doing any active church work. By writing an open pastoral letter the former clergyman Otto Dibelius, contrary to orders, performed active pastoral service. I therefore demand the highest sentence the Court can decree for an insurgent who is unwilling to see that his activity is a danger and his assumed service a real disservice to the German nation."

The accused was permitted to say two sentences to both indictments. "What do you say," the attorney asked, "to the indictment of pastoral service where service was strictly forbidden to you?"

To this question, the accused had only one short answer:

A Christian is never off duty. I serve Christ wherever I can. The only question worth raising is whether the faithful of Germany can still live up to the apostle's saying, "We should obey God rather than men."

The attorney, an elderly official called Wesenberg, had another question to ask: "What have you to say to the false statement that the Reich minister denied Jesus Christ being the Son of God?"

Dibelius answered:

Four hundred and fifty leading Nazi officials have heard the Minister for Religious Affairs saying this: "To maintain the divinity of Christ is ridiculous." Here is the list of the four hundred and fifty officials present at the minister's proclamation of new worship outlines. I would like to ask each of the four hundred and fifty for his testimony. If there is any contra-

diction in their witness, I shall produce a statement signed by two former party commissioners present at the proclamation and setting forth clearly what the Reich minister said on that occasion.

Here the Reich minister collapsed and was hurried into seclusion away from the gaze of onlookers. Attorney Wesenberg declared Dibelius acquitted, stating that the case would be reopened only if the accused should fail to stop the distribution of the open letter he had written to Minister Kerrl.

The German press was censored; the British and American were not. Leading newspapers of the English Commonwealth, the United States, and Latin America reprinted the open letter. Thousands of copies flooded Germany. Nazi censorship this time proved inefficient; it could not even demonstrate that the man who wrote the letter had been instrumental in its worldwide distribution.

Seen from the outside, Dibelius had done very little. He had only written what he had experienced with the Christ whom he called his brother. With a simple human instinct for the basic realities of situation and character, he won a victory, and he won it by being just himself. To him life was service with Christ.

To the men of brilliant bigness and burning blood, life was something very different—a dream of material power and pride. Their love was only self-seeking. Life in its deeper expressions, however, the life of sacrificial love and sharing, was on the side of the "former clergyman," the disfrocked leader of the young, the watchman in the night, the heir to ancient knights in order, the partner and brother of Christ.

Greetings were sent from all corners of Europe to congratulate the defender of Protestant freedom on his stern and able witness. Yet Dibelius knew how important it was that he for one should not lose the sense of urgency in a mental and spiritual fight of world-wide dimensions. He was determined to make his partnership with Christ real in full obedience and fidelity. He was the last to suffer from delusions of grandeur. No cross no crown—such was the true line of Protestant pilgrims.

In his life this was the period when Hitler, so far the greatest

of this century's pagan usurpers, became interested in more
subtle methods for doing away with the man who had made his
close accomplice Kerrl collapse in a court. The leader encouraged Kerrl to approach Goering who was then in charge of the
ghastly concentration camps. Goering, however, knew from his
Scandinavian relatives how great the churchman's reputation
already was outside Germany. He declined to sign an order of
concentration for custody. At present, Kerrl could just take a
cruel revenge on Wesenberg before he stirred Hitler again in his
fury. Judge Wesenberg died from the consequences of the minister's reprisals within a year's space. Then the time seemed ripe
for prosecuting Dibelius once more. He had been seen in pastoral and administrative action several miles from his gloomy
residence. He had opened an office for clergy and laymen in resistance to terror, jointly with Pastor Curt Scharf whom he
trusted and treated as a friend.

Suddenly rearrested, Dibelius was brought to Alexanderplatz
Gaol, where torture chambers were close at hand whenever
hearings seemed uncommonly lengthy to those eager for finish-
ing verdicts quickly. There is insufficient evidence as to how far
Hitler himself was behind the third action taken against Dibelius. The hearings were most thorough, but suddenly ended.
The reason was wholly unexpected.

The United States Embassy communicated to "the former
clergyman now under political investigation" a registered letter
from Dr. Samuel D. Press, president of Eden Theological Seminary. The letter was a brotherly expression of solidarity and
goodwill toward "a German citizen whose work has done the
greatest honor to the name of the German nation in the new
world." Attached to the letter was a resolution of the Eden authorities to confer an honorary doctor's degree on the undaunted
hero of Germany's Protestant tradition.

No more hearings, no more open cruelty. The diplomatic
relations with the United States and the maintaining of cultural
bonds with America's Protestant churches were still more vital
than the total suppression of what was historically the mother
church of the Reformation.

The disfrocked pastor was now permitted a less restricted but still rather carefully watched range of activity. Never again was he to drive over all the visiting area. The services in which he ventured to preach and administer the sacraments were not to be announced in public for some years to come. When he joined the faithful in Dahlem's Church of St. Anne to lead in prayer and intercession for Martin Niemoeller, at that time under investigation and soon to be transferred to concentration camp, only the very regular churchgoer would know that here again was the place where Otto Dibelius gave his heart and soul. Candidates for ordination were anxious indeed to begin their ministry under the hands of their truthful earthly shepherd. But the doors had to be locked when the service lasted long and too many were streaming in to take Holy Communion with the pastor of pastors.

For the sake of his family, he was glad to leave that apartment over the garage at last. But it was no honest relief that was offered to him. The residence now assigned to him and his ailing wife toward the end of the war was damp and dark and dreary in all aspects. The bedroom was actually located below the ground at Lichterfelde. When the greater part of that suburb was bombed by the Allies and, a year later, finished off by retreating Nazis, frail Mrs. Dibelius would join the neighboring women bravely engaged in cleaning up and removing the outward ravages of mass destruction.

The actual decision as to who was to lose the second war had fallen at least three years before that spring-cleaning of 1945. In fact, the verdict against the devilish aspirations of the "magnetic" Reich leader had been passed in the spring of 1933 when, a month after Hitler's usurpation, Otto Dibelius wrote the following words in the first of the pastoral letters leading up to his twelve years' ostracism:

Let us maintain that in the gospel there is no respect for high and mighty persons, but only for sinners justified by faith. The kingdom of God is the subject of our preaching, but never the glory of one particular race or blood. The gospel of Christ is op-

posed to any self-sufficient ideology whether nationalist or social-
ist, liberal or conservative. Community and state, political free-
dom and the many more human attainments will be in their
proper place only when reconciled with the gospel of Christ.
The true church of Christ can never allow the claims of human
beings to pass without their rededication to God's holy will.

An enormous amount of thought and will power had been
wasted to erase the name of Christ, the will of God, from Europe's historical records. The foreign usurper had abused the
message of the church for more than twelve years of German
rule. His mask had been that of an all-world liberator. Now it
was stripped off under the eyes of those who, apparently, had
not prayed in vain.

But was it freedom that the Allied forces brought in the
name of Christ? They said so in some of their official radio
broadcasts in the German language. Was Europe's reconstruction discussed in an atmosphere of forgiveness and mutual confidence when Hitler's body had been drenched with petrol and
burnt in the courtyard of Berlin's collapsing chancellery? No,
Berlin's reappointed spiritual leader found the atmosphere of
the whole continent poisoned and utterly disgraceful.

Steward W. Herman, the American Lutheran who spent the
greater part of the Nazi era in the heart of Berlin, has accurately
described how, just a week after Hitler's suicide, Otto Dibelius
"emerged from the catacombs of Berlin to become the Confessing Synod's Protestant Bishop."[3] The episcopal title, established
with allied approval, was a source of discomfort to some few
among the German pastors. They were those who felt that the
depravity of Nazi actions had been so monstrous that stains
were left on the name of everyone and everything German,
making the whole nation an accomplice to the damage done in
the countries occupied, such as Czechoslovakia, Yugoslavia,
Greece, the Benelux countries, France, Denmark, and Norway.

---

[3] Steward W. Herman, *The Rebirth of the German Church*, p. 93.
Harper, 1946.

Against the background of all that had happened in the war-stricken countries, some of Germany's confessing church party would carry the feeling of collective guilt very far. They wished to have excluded, once and for ever, any possibility of a Germany resuming her traditional tendencies, including the fateful complex that she occupied the center position on the continent. Quite a few of the confessing party leaders demanded that the ordering and shaping of German cultural life, including that of the church, should be left entirely to the four Big Powers to whom victory was given by God's providence, as they understood it.

As the German school of idealism had deteriorated a considerable time ago, so the confessing party leaders thought that the realm of the inner spirit should henceforth attract only subordinate interest. The whole of Immanuel Kant's time-honored philosophy, the postulate of free-will decision, was abandoned. All the means of extricating individual human beings from deterministic conclusions were discarded with a vigor which only German intellectuals were likely to produce. The rigid dogma of predestination was re-established complete with all the rational rules of causation. It was a sad return to the life and thought-forms of the late sixteenth century when the school of Calvin was putting more coercion into human existence than any of the great Reformers would ever have agreed to.

But Dibelius felt strongly that the trend toward coercion and the outlawing of man's God-given freedom must not go unchecked:

Let us return to the gospel of Christ. His message does not follow the currents of outward events. The glorious liberty of the children of God is not to perish with the pagan dream of man's self-perfection through blood and race.

So at a time when the free decision of individual man was ridiculed and even besmirched, when the rigid expounders of predestination joined hands with the advocates of milieu materialism, Berlin's new bishop reformulated an exposition of Christian liberty based on the finest of early scriptural thinkers:

As a child of God and a brother of Christ, I own the spirit of freedom. To this spirit I am committed wholly with body and mind. I will live and die for this freedom. I desire to have it brought back to many more children of God. For every one of them is a personality whose aim it is to lead a full life according to the holy secret given to him through the process of creation, interacting in his soul and in his body. Let each man have the chance to develop his deep inward design. Let him never, not even in his bodily action, forget who was his Designer, a very personal being indeed.

The human individual, do not reduce it by force. Do not strive to make individual man uniform with his neighbor, not even with his brother. The true Father likes his children growing different and independent. He likes them free. That is why I am committed to freedom, and I feel sure that many more children of God will gladly live and die for that glorious freedom.

CHAPTER TEN

Late Night Curtain

THE MAN who held the banner of man's individual freedom high, was also strong enough to raise the lowered impulses of his defeated nation to a vision of light and a new commitment to life and corporate action. He had no illusions about the faultiness of the human species, least of all about the potential of the Nordic or German race. Yet he believed firmly in the new creation[1] with its transforming of the crude aggressive instincts in the human self. He knew through his own experience the reality of a life transformed in Christ. With this experience, he did not nurture nostalgic sentiments over what reactionaries called the good old times:

History is largely a succession of broken shrines and dismantled images. Yet within that perennial process of self-deception and annihilation, the church's birthright is to share, to heal, and to reconcile.

The healing of a nation can be brought about only by making the thickly covered wellsprings flow again with living waters, leaving it to the Creator and Preserver to direct the waters into brooks or streams.

---

[1] 2 Cor. 5:17.

No man is perfect and fit enough to establish absolute values by himself. Nor is any group of human beings, whether a western nation or an eastern classless society, justified in denying to a unit less strenuous than itself, the inherited cultural identity.

Observing the victorious powers as they lined up to form the United Nations, Otto Dibelius discovered among them such deeply divergent trends that he could not help wondering whether they would be instrumental in providing freedom for a wholesome Christian church. And only a free and independent church could give herself to the great new task of sharing and healing:

The process of healing is seldom furthered by force. Healing is a miraculous process in which some persons of faith and patience may participate; it is not an overnight process. To be healed means to be deeply and fully restored to the freedom to live up to the Maker's image.

The freedom promised to the children of God is nowhere in Holy Scripture said to be abstract. The freedom of God's design is as tangible as it is open to improper use. It is just as concrete as the fact that God's own Son is the son of man, tempted, suffering, and struggling as other human beings.

"The son of man is come to seek and to save that which was lost." There is no nation so forsaken or so depraved that it might not retain some part of its original mission also to be instrumental in the unfolding of God's grace and goodwill to men of other nations.

Like an answer to the Bishop's faith in the incarnate Son of God as our true brother, there came to him and his fellow-workers a heartening expression of Christian brotherhood when the World Council sent eight delegates to Stuttgart in October, 1945 in order to receive a Declaration of Responsibility and Repentance from the new all-German church council, of which Bishop Dibelius was a member. The declaration included these words:

We are deeply grateful for this visit from the World Council of Churches, for we know ourselves to be one with our people

*in a great company of suffering and in a great solidarity of guilt.
True, we have struggled for many years in the name of Jesus
Christ against a spirit which found its terrible expression in the
National Socialist regime of violence, but we accuse ourselves
for not witnessing more courageously, for not praying more
faithfully, for not believing more joyously, and for not loving
more ardently. Now a new beginning is to be made in our
churches. That in this new beginning we may be aware of our
wholehearted unity with the other churches of the ecumenical
fellowship fills us with deep joy. We hope in God that through
the common service of the churches, the spirit of violence and
revenge which again today tends to become powerful may be
brought under control in the whole world.*

Among the eight World Council representatives were two
fine men whose particular concern was the search for some
true essence of love buried beneath the ruins of Europe. In
their earnest quest for Europe's soul, they wished to avoid the
danger that this historic occasion in Stuttgart might end in
bitter and fruitless recrimination. They were Bishop George
Bell of Chichester and Samuel McCrea Cavert of America's
Federal Council. Both of them recalled the German resisters'
first Declaration of Responsibility, drawn up during 1942 in
the alcove of a Freiburg professor's private residence. At that
time Hitler was still much in his glory and strength.

To independent onlookers from abroad, the Alcove Declaration was a witness brave enough to prove the sincerity of Dibelius and his co-authors, who were now only repeating what
they had written three years earlier and managed to send to
their brothers abroad.

In the late summer of 1945, Central Europe was the area
which the four victorious powers decreed must be divided into
curtained zones. It was also the scene of an advance of the West
to a considerable extent negated and undone. Owing to the lack
of a European program and European leadership, Germany was
very much the "house divided against itself."

There were misguided German critics whose lack of historic

perspective led them to play havoc with an antiquated theology of the cross that left out faith in resurrection and ascension. Moreover, there were those of the younger generation who had resisted Hitler and who now turned to the new Bishop of Berlin with these questions: Where is our share of the fruits of victory over the pseudo-religious dictator? Where is the promise of freedom fulfilled? Did Hitler's dictatorship cease only to make room for world revolution as it is now heralded by the commanders of the Red Army? Dibelius gave answer to these questions when he preached his first sermon in a public service after twelve years of enforced silence.

The text he chose was from the Old Testament—the sober and solid words of Moses, the liberator of God's people, leading them through the desert and destined to see the land of his fathers from afar. To the faithful and truly repentant it would be given to see that beloved land restored to its earlier commitment:

> Thou shalt do that which is right and good in the sight of the Lord, that thou mayest go in and possess the good land which the Lord sware unto thy fathers. And to thy son thou shalt say, We were Pharaoh's bondmen in Egypt, and the Lord brought us out of Egypt with a mighty hand (Deuteronomy 6:18, 21).

Applying this ancient command and the parallel pledge from the thirteenth chapter of the Book of Exodus to the position of his defeated and largely displaced people in 1945, Otto Dibelius said:

Hitler's defeat means nothing less and nothing more than this: The Confessing Church has not perished in the desert. The pilgrim people of God have been led a part of the promised way to freedom. VE Day, however, is not what Moses and the prophets called the acceptable time, ushering in the day of salvation. We shall look up again to the Lord going before us by night in a pillar of fire.

It is true that today we can gather within open doors. Yet we shall continue to be a wandering people—we cannot rest nor bury ourselves in the past.

The sense of wholeness and oneness with God, that sense of certainty which grew in our time of testing, is not to fade away. Nor shall the spirit of God's pilgrim people lose its vigor by restoring an order dating from disspirited periods when almost everything was taken for granted and no great things were expected from him who will yet return to judge the quick and the dead.

The nearer now the hour of final parting and sifting comes, the greater will be the signs attending those who look forward in steadfastness. They shall speak with new tongues.

Let us, therefore, praise the true Judge and Savior with new hymns of adoration, not based on illusions, but on reality. It would be fatal indeed to re-establish the churches as they were when the Nazi usurpers made us their bondmen. The time is past in which we could tolerate the church's historical dependence on the mighty of the earth.

The rightful way to make the life of Christian people a clean and honest enterprise has always been the simple way of sharing and mutual giving. Few people knew better than the newly appointed bishop that the shaping of a corporate life with Christ is largely an outcome of personal encounters.

At moments of history the God who meets man in a personal, direct, and simple way has also found his aping counterpart. Reviewing the European church situation of 1945, one is tempted to assume that Satan also makes some men respond in a very personal and congenial way. The most elaborate of the infernal tempter's designs is surely his art of indictment and recrimination.

The dramatizing of a sad spectacle thus became the great temptation of 1945 and afterward. The German Christians' outcries of self-indictment had more than theological interest. They ushered in a whole range of historical studies. It could no longer be ignored that the whole turnover of the Nazis was but one step along the course of world revolution set by German citizens in the nineteenth century. Marx and Engels had worked out their outlines for such a revolution in the bosom of the great Mother Germania. At a later time Lenin himself had been given the privileged use of a German imperial railroad car to enter Russia for setting the Communist revolt in full motion.

All this was vehemently recalled in the frustrated Germans' vocal lamentations. Onlookers who based their philosophy on the strange phenomena of man's outward existence found the doors wide open to welcome studies in resentment. In the general affliction there was none of the expected help from the philosophers' angle when the leading existentialist Karl Jasper had the English edition of his essay on *The Spirit of Europe* published with this foreword:

Germany's European monuments are ruins and its intellectual streams have almost petered out in the burning and dreary sands of nihilism.

What a real comfort it was that some Christians of the Anglo-Saxon world showed a more imaginative and constructive spirit, groping for a fresh understanding of God's design and man's disorder. They were not heirs of saintly tradition blind to the urgent need for Christian solidarity in that desperate hour. Otto Dibelius would never forget how George Bell of Chichester and three equally ecumenically-minded Americans helped create a new climate in which the weakened and despondent were not altogether banished from the healing rays of the light. What a challenge was in that change of climate and horizon! He had hardly expected ever to breathe that different atmosphere again. How forceful and fascinating was the revealing of the errors of the self-righteous! How suddenly clear it became that with the destruction of Central Europe *all* concepts of the West were being defied!

One of the finest Christians whom Otto Dibelius met at that time was Francis Pickens Miller, a colonel in the first unit to set up the United States Military Government in Berlin. In the late fall of 1945, his office building was not far away from the bishop's house. It was sixteen years since the two men had last met. In 1929, Miller had visited Berlin as the General Secretary of the World's Student Christian Federation. At that time, Dibelius was still very much the "leader of the young." Now he was suffering from the consequences of three arrests, eighteen months of hunger, and agitation about his wife whose health was to be a prolonged source of disturbance to him.

Francis Pickens Miller managed to bring to the Bishop's house parcels of excellent food and medical supplies. Dibelius accepted the first of those parcels for his wife. When more of them arrived, he asked the generous colonel for permission to share with a friend who was in still greater need than he and his wife.

Miller was delighted to hear the name of the man about whom the Bishop was now so deeply concerned. It was none other than Reinold von Thadden. Also three times arrested by the Nazis, von Thadden had seen the fourth and worst of his periods in prison near Archangelsc, the distant arctic harbor. Like a skeleton and covered with symptoms of a grave disease yet to be identified, he was sent back by the Soviets to be healed or to die at home. However, his home estate in Pomerania was just as ransacked as had been Dibelius' early Pomeranian parishes. Reinold, the heir of one of East Germany's most renowned nobility, was transported to Berlin. So utterly frail and discouraged did he arrive here, that he was laid up for a long time in an invalids' home.

Invalids' homes were dreary abodes in the hungry city of 1945 and 1946. The good Samaritan was, therefore, all the happier to look after the comrade of his earlier years. For like the American colonel, Reinhold von Thadden was a long-time officer of the Student Christian Movement. It took months of nursing and good feeding before he could leave his sickbed. When he could walk again, he was still fearfully reluctant to move toward the safer west of Germany through the Soviet zone by means of public transportation. But Francis Miller knew better ways of traffic without infringing on the allied regulations. And there were good ambulance men in the American army.

Reinold von Thadden, the honored veteran and leader of the

older student generation, was enabled to make his abode at last in Fulda, the city of St. Boniface and cradle of western Europe's Christendom. Two Christian brothers had literally saved from early death the man for whom the great Designer had still reserved the noble task of ushering in the continental movement of Kirchentag.

This laymen's movement was for a long time "to save the church of our century from developing a fixed resistance to tackling new problems." Von Thadden, the coming President of Kirchentag and chairman of the committee for the Laymen's Institute at Bossey, Switzerland, was indeed for Bishop Dibelius a God-given guardian of the church in action. As long as this valiant leader of the lay people was alive and at work, the Bishop could hope that his flock and fold would be a forward-looking church. Onlookers of a less sympathetic heart than Francis Miller had shown might well have been satisfied to see the German church fall back into traditional and even outmoded ways of existence.

Dibelius gladly put his trust in von Thadden as an ally. He was convinced that his friend, happily restored to health, would make Kirchentag a rallying point for all new impulses toward lay responsibility. Kirchentag should be a movement and not just another institution. It should enlarge cooperation between clergy and laymen, and become a truly ecumenical fellowship for ordinary people.

The first postwar Kirchentag rally was planned to be held in Essen, deep in the industrial Ruhr district. Much of von Thadden's early experience with student volunteers went into the preparatory work to which he gave almost three years.

A spirit of brotherly encounter and personal venture changed the whole church scene. In the fall of 1947, Otto Dibelius found himself encouraged to speak to audiences very different from the prewar clerical conferences of the old world. The man who welcomed him back to the new world was the same servant of the coming united church who had greeted him in 1921, Louis W. Goebel. Joining him now in his greeting of hearty welcome were two more pioneers of Christian solidarity, the Federal Council's

Samuel McCrea Cavert and Henry Smith Leiper. They had studied and circulated the German church's declarations of repentance. Taking those statements of 1942 and 1945 at their real value, they were detached and strong enough to advise the leaders of a "reborn church" not to repeat declarations of repentance too frequently, lest these should be misconstrued and exploited for political purposes.[2]

It was a happy experience to see America again after more than a quarter of a century filled with Europe's struggle and defeat. New York had grown immensely and almost fearfully. But the lovely stretches of dear old Pennsylvania were almost the same as in 1921. He spoke mainly to young people now. Cedar Crest College at Allentown and Albright College at Reading gave him warm reception. J. Arthur Heck, then president of the Evangelical United Brethren Seminary at Reading, acted both as a generous host and a loving brother. Quite unexpectedly, the Bishop felt spiritually at home among a people faithfully holding to their Pennsylvania Dutch idiom, which was really the German way of talking in the Palatinate. Nobler and deeper elements of that area's heritage were recalled as the Bishop drove past the beautiful towns named Bethlehem, Nazareth, Emmaus, and New Jerusalem. Could a land with such an array of rural and industrial towns go the way of all flesh? Was there not something magnificently, indestructibly alive in the William Penn looking down from his City Hall on the precincts of his holy enterprise, on that city whose name was conceived ages before America was established? Indeed Dibelius would always cherish the supernal sight of the garden city surrounding the Independence Hall, this unforgettable city of loyal brotherly love rightly called Philadelphia.

The month was October. German-speaking folk attended him on his way from William Penn's fair city to the less prepossessing triangle of Pittsburgh. They asked him to participate in a com-

---

[2] In his sermon on Acts 5:34-41, held in St. Mary's, East Berlin, on June 7, 1953 Bishop Dibelius referred in detail to the American churchmen advising him not to repeat the declarations of repentance too often.

memoration of Wittenberg's auspicious day, the last of October. The request resulted in the first ecumenical service held by all the major churches of the triangle. In the city of McKeesport they worshiped together to honor God's great gift of Martin Luther's Reformation. A second and similar occasion followed when the Bishop was invited to Martin Luther Memorial Place in Washington, D. C. Here the American Lutheran churches gave splendid proof of their new partnership in ecumenical co-operation.

Pennsylvania still retained her traditional appointed place as a bridge connecting the new world with the old world of Dibelius. How essential it seemed to him to widen that bridge and to fortify it for the years to come.

Coming from freedom's new outpost in the heart of ancient Europe, he was rightly in search of the deepest purpose abiding in the soul of America. How impressive that country's power appeared to him. But how, he would ask, was that power related to the universal values which surely America was holding in trust for all mankind? As the century was nearing its zenith, was America's past but a prologue? Might not the coming great day bring about a grander consummation of the destinies of all nations?

America's enthusiasm was as great and as marvelous as ever. How splendid, how almost irritating her efficiency! What a whirlwind of pilot projects not only advertised in gay colors, but actually unfolding and reaching out into the future!

When was the acceptable hour to come in which the past would ever be present and the future no more a distant kind of utopia? The contemporary sky was still thickly covered with clouds. The heart of Europe, the eastern homeland to which the Bishop returned in the late November of 1947 seemed little more in Advent mood and festive expectation than it had been in the two previous winter seasons. No peace treaty was ever in sight. History, made without the Son of Man, was taking her revenge, displaying all her desperate logic. This was not a time to love and renew.

And yet a new day was destined to come. Nearing too was the

hour "when Protestants of East and Central Europe would awaken to find themselves vital elements of a movement for world renewal." America, ever so young and ever so challenging, had opened new and wide perspectives to the traveler's responsive mind. In no way tired by the autumnal ocean voyage, he set to work at once relating his renewed encounter with the new world's Protestantism to the finality of all that history could mean when seen with the living Christ.

The good German came to realize how widely and greatly the focus of historic life was moving. Europe, the old world, was no longer isolated from the new. The task of European reconstruction was no longer a matter of self defense. God's ultimate appeal was directed at greater and much wider shores. He saw the new reality of interrelated lands and converging seas.

As he set out to explore to the full that new reality, he was reminded irresistibly of the very first sermon he had preached to his own people one night in 1945 when the iron curtain had fallen over his wounded land. Yet how much less dreary, how much more hopeful the same words sounded now:

The nearer the hour of final parting and sifting comes, the greater will be the signs attending those who look forward in steadfastness. They shall speak with new tongues.

Let us, therefore, praise the true Judge and Savior with new hymns of adoration, not based on illusions, but on reality. It would be fatal indeed to re-establish the churches as they were when the Nazi usurpers made us their bondmen. The time is past in which we could tolerate the church's historical dependence on the mighty of the earth.

The one hymn which Otto Dibelius created for the younger groups of the Confessing Church, set to his own music, was a passionate prayer:[3]

---

[3] The author is indebted to the Rev. E. G. Marrison of Kuala Lampur, Malaya, for English adaptations to pieces from the Confessional Hymnary, Wehr and Waffen.

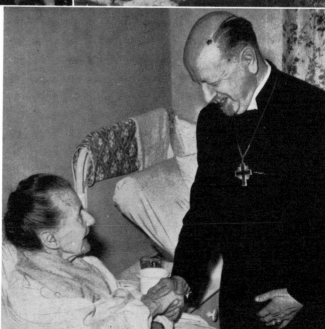

Above, preaching in
East Berlin's Cathe-
dral of St. Mary;
New Year's Day,
1956

Above right, laying
foundation stone for
first wooden church
in war-damaged Ber-
lin; Spring 1954

Right, Otto Dibelius
visiting in Oberlin-
Babelsberg, Soviet-
controlled Home for
Invalids; Winter
1955

Press-Foto

Otto Dibelius and granddaughter Irmgard; May 1955

Saying farewell to Julius Bodensieck, U.S. Protestant Liaison Representative, and Mrs. Bodensieck, Welfare Officer for Baltic Displaced Persons, Lübeck; 1953

Religious News Service

Let not, oh God, the fiendish tempter with us stay.
Cast not thy people, not our lives, our broken souls away.
Save us who vainly filled the holy wine in bottles old.
   Redeem us from evil friends in our testing time
   and in the judgment thou alone wilt rightly hold.
Let Christ, our brother, do the healing work of radiant
   renewal.
Let him then be our shield, our crown of righteousness,
   our jewel.
Give us thy armor, only once more to rejoice
   that we may utter with the last endowment of our voice:
Thou, Lord, art with us in our depth and surely in our radiant
   morning.
Until it comes in full, we wait in patience and in faithful
   expectation.
   Through all our night we watch,
   our hearts thy throne adorning,
Until in clarity thy light, thy day is dawning.

CHAPTER ELEVEN

Salt of the Earth

It was quite clear to Dibelius that in the present century there was no possibility of any comeback for a church dependent on the agents of earthly rule and power. No spiritual leader could help the long misguided people of Central Europe to discern the signs of the times if he compromised with the crude and perverted instincts of material power and domination.

At the right moment true men of God appeared in Germany. Three of them, different in temper, had come through utterly divergent experiences. There was the old and pious Theophil Wurm of Stuttgart. He had followed a call to Wittenberg in 1934 when Hitler wished a bishop of the Kerrl type[1] consecrated there in the rites of the blood-and-race religion. The eleven years that followed were spent by Wurm in a wail of penitence and a nation-wide self-reproach.

The second leader for the church's rethinking was Martin

---

[1] The Nazi Reich's bishop, former army chaplain Ludwig Mueller, made the National Synod at Wittenberg, August 1934, propose that each German pastor should swear an oath of spiritual loyalty to Hitler and an explicit renunciation of the non-Nazi church government of Dibelius. Concerning Reich Minister Kerrl, cf. chapter 9.

Niemoeller, who had taken the road "from Uboat to pulpit" and suffered more than six years in concentration camp for his renunciation of all militant ways of self-support.

Otto Dibelius was the third man in the group committed to the work of Christian reconstruction in Germany. He "emerged from the catacombs," it is true. He had not been a partner, not even an unwilling one, in the blasphemous desecration of Luther's Wittenberg.

The place where Wurm, Niemoller, Dibelius, and others met to join forces was Treysa, the western Hessians' Protestant Home for Invalids, now overflooded with mothers on trek and children born in exile. Dibelius seemed to have brought with him all the living horror and heartbreaking misery of those eastern areas which he was to represent in the new church administration.

But what was the significance of the East, thoroughly ransacked by an Allied army and now offered to be sacrificed, with Yalta's blessings, for pacifying another totalitarian deity? After all—and this was a fateful question for a Christian loyal to the land of his fathers—what was the major part of East Germany for many years? Was it not just Prussia, that Protestant kingdom rightly ridiculed by the more polished types of intellectuals? Had Protestant East Germany ever really been integrated into that aristocratic order of bygone centuries about which all Catholics and quite a few Lutherans were so nostalgic? No, this was rough and dour and mocked-at Prussia. Nothing holy about her in the sense of the prestige-ridden Holy Roman Empire! The saintliness of the East was the less ostentatious kind befitting a sober watchman whose attention belongs to the hours of the night.

For the appointed watchman in the night, this was not yet the historic hour to plead with the Catholics. The more urgent preparation for all-German daylight work was some satisfactory settlement with the traditional Lutheran units of Western Hanover and Bavaria.

Dibelius made it clear to many, if not to all in Germany, that Martin Luther was greater in mind and wider in heart than some contemporary confessionalists appeared to be with their magic and their mosaic of Luther's words:

If we wish to do honor to Luther, let us return to the God of history. It was the living God whose spirit guides us into all the truth, it was the God in process of continuing action, who was Luther's strength and his stay.

We are doing ill to perpetuate Luther's special devices in a given situation. We are not fought by the Turks as was the Holy Empire of Luther's time. Our challenge is the new world power and world philosophy of world revolution.

As our surroundings have changed in their reality, so also our ways of dealing with them, our very thought forms have become different from those of our fathers in the sixteenth century. That doesn't mean our fathers were wrong. Much less does it mean that Luther's approach to the tremendous task of his great century was in any way a failure.

Dibelius had something to say to the intellectuals too:

Don't make an orthodox scheme of categories out of the man called Luther. If you read his sayings with your heart, if you read not only his academic lectures, you will find how gloriously he escapes the rigid recasting of his thoughts into schemes or skeletons of lifeless awe.

I have found life in Luther as it is. I have found some remarkable contradictions in his writings, and I am not so afraid of them as the orthodox and the perfectionists are. Luther wasn't perfect. Nor would the church of his age have called him orthodox.

There is just too much sophistry among orthodox theologians. I find it quite amazing. Our time of testing is hardly over, and now these intellectuals harden their hearts again and blunt their thoughts. Their rendering of the things on which we would set our affection becomes so vague and shallow.

We were not sustained by sophistical arguing when we were in the cells or prison yards.

I have come to hate sophistical arguing and speculative reasoning just as I feel a pity for all sophisticated persons. Isn't there something horrible about the person who is always right? Is there anything of the child of God left in the sophisticated?

I for one prefer to admit that I am very often wrong. But then I always rejoice that I belong to those who have been born again of incorruptible seed.

For whole centuries the history of German Christendom with its twofold streams—Lutheranism on the one side, the enthusiasts and the later confessing church party on the other—was largely the story of lost balance. Balance was indeed lost rather early. Seeking now to restore it was a surprisingly small number of church leaders as the twentieth of the Christian centuries was nearing its zenith.

The Treysa Conference of 1945 showed a keen desire on the part of the Lutherans to have a federation of churches. They felt, however, that such a federation should be governed by more than the three leaders mentioned above—Wurm, Niemoeller, and Dibelius. Twelve seemed to them a minimum number. With the twelve would come the whole pattern of confessional dispute with its weighty logic superceding both comprehensiveness and balance.

Reasoning and the mere logic of facts are seldom sufficient where tensions are the outgrowth of unforgiven sins. And there were unforgiven sins resulting in a straining of conscience on more than one side of the antagonizing parties and confessions.

To escape the atmosphere of tension, the more devout among the German Lutherans went back to bury their souls deep in the hollows of individual edification. But the men of Treysa thought a return to the romantic kind of pietism incompatible with the newly accepted responsibility for a wholesome church in a regenerated nation.

What then was to come of the conventicle piety much in vogue in some southern and western areas of Germany? Was that pious practice of *edification* worth remolding and restoring to its biblical reality?

Dibelius was ready to appreciate *edification* where it was reassessed as the building of a corporate unit out of living stones:

Where living stones are put together, there everyone grows to fit into his own place and helps his neighbor to fit into his,

within the great design. It is from the foundation and the cor-
ner stone that our whole life, as a harmonious structure knit
together by the joints with which it is provided, grows by the
proper functioning of individual parts to its full maturity in
love.[2]

His search for living stones was pathetic indeed. He did not
really find them among backward-minded contemporaries:

What ineffectual qualities have these pietists managed to at-
tach to their edifying characters? I can see how disgusted our
struggling young people are with the exhibitionism displayed
by those characters. In the basic biblical sense of the term, they
are not edifying at all. They are edified, but only by their self-
assertiveness. They attempt to monopolize the Bible, and what
is worse, they use the idiom of that holy Book as if there existed
an authorized version of man's earthly way to perfection. I honestly admit I have no place for their forbidding airs of piety.
Nor is their private language intelligible to those who had to
meet the living Christ in war trenches and isolation camps, at
the very frontier of modern man's existence.

Surely this postwar period was the time when the Christian
communities of Western Germany should replace their several arguments of convention and wonted use with a frontier
spirit animated by a nationwide responsibility. It was at Treysa
that Dibelius underlined a saying of William Temple:

Christianity is either to rediscover its material impact on
the nature of persons and their material resources, or else it
will leave mankind to the brutal realization of a different materialism whose vulgar predictions are before us.

Berlin's bishop initiated rebuilding at the very foundation of
Lutheran church life. He gave a new impulse to a pastoral and
professorial commission to issue a revised text of Luther's Bible,

---

[2] Otto Dibelius said this in German when he spoke on the Keyword of
the Year at Kirchentag in Essen. For the rendering in English, J. B. Phil-
lips' congenial translation has been used with the references to 1 Peter 2
and Ephesians 4.

much to the surprise and anger of the newly rising dictators, Hitler's successors in the East. They envisaged dangers to their soul-capturing philosophy if young Germans were given an opportunity to read the message of Christ in modern terms. In the thirties Dibelius' mimeographed worship aids had been suspect on account of their daringly up-to-date language. Now he was giving to the new generation of postwar pastors brilliant examples of expounding God's word to all kinds of listeners, especially to those reluctant to breathe the traditional stuffy atmosphere of ivory towers.

The Bishop did not let the eventful year of 1945 pass without making it known that he needed the support of inspired interpreters of God's word in order to bring that word nearer to the heart of modern man. Dietrich Bonhoeffer, poet, writer, and the Confessing Church's profoundest and most eloquent adviser in the field of pastoral messages, had died as a martyr. It would be difficult to replace him. Hermann Strathmann of Erlangen, an able linguist and a public speaker in the good old Stoecker tradition, tried his best. It would be no easy task to find the fine balance between that archaic beauty of language which is apt to lull the intellect, and that modern factualness which often involves the danger of minimizing and blunting the greatness of God's mighty acts on earth.

That balance would be found by one whose cultural attainment was a strong feeling for the mystical and creative element in man's living speech. Dibelius' early research in the field of ritual and music moved him to emphasize that language was in itself an issue of life. And to him there was no fruitful issue where beauty, truth, and charity were kept apart. In good time the noble work was begun, with all the hope and confidence of Christian people whose deepest searchings were to be reconceived and restated in their mother tongue. Over ten years would pass before Dibelius himself set the final seal to the Revised Standard Version of Luther's Holy Bible.

The year was still 1945. Two country pastors who had a chance to greet their bishop in the afternoon of Christmas Day found him sitting over a pot of hot turnip water and slices of

thinly spread corn bread while his wife had one cup of real
tea and two buttered biscuits in bed. That much he had retained from a huge parcel sent to him by one of his prewar
Swedish friends.

His living room and his study were unheated. Those were
still the basement rooms allotted to him by the Nazis. In the
damp bedroom where his wife had decorated a silvery tree of
celestial morning beauty, some real warmth and radiant light
were beaming from candles made in Sweden, matchless in their
thin and tender length like those rays unending in a Northern Swedish summer night.

A new year was coming, a year in which the western Allies
envisaged real peace for Germany. Berlin's bishop felt the call
to comfort and encourage many of his people. As he read out
the lesson of the eighth day after Christmas, the story of old
Simeon waiting in the temple for his fallen nation's consolation,[3] he represented himself as a true follower of that lonely
waiting prophet, and included in the waiting company those
who came in between, the multitudes whose names he knew
to be written in heaven. This was the first of many festive seasons in which the Bishop was destined to think silently of his
own sons' unknown graves.

His deep and searching thoughts made all his sermon on that
New Year's Day ring out as a prayer:

In our day, hearts are often so hardened and embittered that
we pray God to give us more yielding hearts, hearts that have
the wish to listen to the other side, to unite those who are at
odds, and to work toward harmony. So much discord will be
carried over from the old year into the new.

It seems more difficult for our people than for any other nation in the world happily to tolerate views other than our own.
In no other nation of the world is pounding the table with
one's fist and tolerating no contradiction considered such a sign
of manly character as it is in ours. One sometimes wishes Mar-

---

[3] Luke 2:25-35.

tin Luther had never spoken his great words at Worms, "Here I stand, I cannot do otherwise," when one sees how many use these words to glorify their own stubbornness. For the new year, let us pray God to give us more compassion and in that compassion a greater steadfastness.

Just as Christ the Son of God became man for the sake of men, for the sake of ourselves, so his church in action is the fellowship of those watching with compassion the tragedy of falling empires. But let us also reassemble as the fellowship of those who overcome the sin of murdering the very best of men. In the last days of the war, the old year took away from us our prophet and poet in prison, Dietrich Bonhoeffer, our Christian brother and friend.

Our time very much resembles the early struggle and the early rise of Christ's apostles. The community of Christian believers was never so enriching and never so genuine and steady as it was under the frightening soldier-emperors in pagan Rome. The church became the church before she assumed political status by the grace of Constantine who was later called the Great.

We might do well to recall that the very cross which we are sometimes tempted to look upon as decorative was in reality a sign of scandal and shame to the multitudes.

We have heard the timely lesson of old Simeon. Surely his waiting for the perfect consolation reveals warmth and fatherly friendliness in truthful adoration. But the old man was also inspired and very right in pointing out that the child of Christmas which he came to caress is set for the fall of many, and for a sign which shall be spoken against.

Of the many who had thus fallen, some were rising again. Dibelius knew that no words were too great to proclaim the actual triumph of the young poet and prophet whose early death was mourned by Europeans of all nations, by all Protestants and many Catholics too. Dietrich Bonhoeffer had been killed by Nazi Storm Guards a few days before American troops liberated his Bavarian concentration camp. As we have seen, he helped Dibelius to prepare worship aids when uncensored sermons were illegal. He had been caught attempting to bring a message of Dibelius' Council to the Bishop of Chichester during the war, while an earlier letter of Dibelius' to Archbishop Temple had been forwarded by a member of the Bonhoeffer group unchecked. Moreover, Bonhoeffer was the founder and leader of the movement called "Common Brotherhood Life for Youth." On the first anniversary of his execution, Dibelius rightly proclaimed that the battle between dictator worship and Christ worship was being won by the purity, simplicity, and steadiness of the martyrs new and old.[4]

The great young martyr had been a scholar with very unorthodox leanings. His name was to live on as that of a humanitarian. Why, Dibelius asked, should the Church Universal shrink from such genuinely human attributes as Christ signified when he called his disciples "friends," and as his apostle again signified when he warned all Christians not to mind high things in self-conceit, but to condescend to men of low estate.[5]

Dibelius was aware that large numbers of people who were still puzzled by the church's antiquated forms of community life did not trust their ears when a churchman addressed them as "friends." But up he went on the platform of a mass meeting of Berlin's unemployed workers, and this is what he had to say to them:

Friends, you are the salt of the earth. But if salt has lost its taste, how shall its saltiness be restored? It is no longer good for anything except to be thrown out and trodden under foot by men.[6]

Are we all going to be thrown out and trodden under foot, you and I? We have lost very much. Most of you have lost your work, a great many have lost their houses, I have lost my two sons, we have all lost a terrible war.

---

[4] Dibelius' words in St. Anne's Church, Dahlem, on the first anniversary of Dietrich Bonhoeffer's martyrdom (after the sermon preached by Eberhard Bethge), April 9, 1946.

[5] Romans 12:16; John 15:14 ff.

[6] Matthew 5:13.

But our fitness, our very saltiness shall be restored. In the holy land where our Lord preached his Sermon on the Mount, salt is used to hold a fire and increase the heat. Coal and wood are as scarce over there as they are in our city now. But salt holds the necessary property to increase the intensity of the fire. So this is what Christ had in mind: Men with warm hearts and loving souls shall be the salt God uses to keep alive the fire without which the world can never reach the goal for which he created it. Now the salt for God's holy fire is there. You will need that fire, for you have a mighty battle on your hands against the soul-killing forces of the East. They utterly deny that man possesses a living soul.

Yet the whole purpose of God's creation is that the soul of man may reach the destination of happiness, the consummation of joy in righteousness. Now don't say you have no place in God's timetable. I can tell from the expressions on your faces that you can stand some warmth, for yourselves, for those left of your families, and surely for some of your neighbors too. And I implore you: Don't let any big managers belittle the craving of your souls, as the propagandists and activists of our now defeated machinery did with all their bragging and barking.

Mind you, all those who are still in war hospitals and in-firmaries are waiting not only for the woolen blankets and love-ly cans which come from America's churches. No, what they need more vitally still is the proof of warmhearted solidarity. There is no genuine social rebirth without a personal rebirth. There will be no light, no happiness in a world which con-tinues to ignore him who set so many souls on fire. All the pagan world, the world before Christ, was a world without love. In the ancient empires it was just as it is practised in some of our modern states, in those soulless monoliths which I am sure you have had more than enough of. If we care for the sick and invalid today, we don't restore their strength just to use them again for class or state performances. No, we rather want to save them from the fate of bitterness, from cold apathy, and from that nihilism which already makes so many of us forget that we were born to be fellow-laborers with God.

So we all still have work to do. You may well belong to those who are tempted to believe that the power of Christ's church has lost her strength and savor in the course of these 1900 years. Yet the fact is that you and I are Christ's church. Let us, therefore, without respect of persons, labor to develop a church where our soul can be lifted up, where worship is no longer that cold and conventional routine you so rightly abhor. No, let it be filled anew with the inner warmth happily known in our forefathers' time. Don't you remember your elders once telling you about it? Well, it was their souls' outreach, the salt and savor of their time. This salt has surely not lost all its power yet.

It is not my right to ask you if each of you belongs to the salt of the earth. I can only ask this of myself in the name of my Savior. But you also are asked by him. And you can answer this question right away, not only with your lips but with your life.

CHAPTER TWELVE

Candles for the Gates of Hell

THE MAN who brought multitudes of disillusioned, frustrated people to rediscover the Creator in whose image they were made would never go back on what he had signed in Germany's Christian Declaration of Repentance. At the same time, he knew that there were forgiving and truly loving brothers in the Western Alliance who would recall such a fact as Reinhold Niebuhr had stated:

There were many more thousands in Europe who did not bow to their knees to Baal than our American Elijah imagined.[1]

Christians of the old world and the new were becoming more and more interdependent. The spirit of a new day was manifest, and Dibelius did not hesitate to set forth a new dimension greatly transcending the character that human existence has in the fallen creation commonly called nature.

He trusted that some Christ-inspired thoughts would help to guide the Big Four. He faithfully pleaded with Europe's new

[1] From The Irony of American History, by Reinhold Niebuhr, p. 67. Scribner, 1952.

masters, rousing their consciences over all the atrocities and miseries which some western intellectuals and the prophets of dialectical materialism labeled "history's inevitability."

Inevitability was never a term of any great meaning for Dibelius. Existentialists and other intellectuals had too often taken "the inevitable" as an excuse for using history as a method of escape from a world unloved and seemingly repulsive to their approach. Dibelius saw the intellectuals of all ages as weak-tempered whenever tests of proved reliability were demanded. He acknowledged the virtue of such a demand, and believed that the household of God was amply equipped to meet it. The leader of the young, the watchman in the night, the defender of the Christian frontier in the east, the affectionate friend and disciple of the most brotherly and warmhearted bishop of the war and the period following the war, Sweden's Nathan Söderblom—he would hardly be the man to depreciate all the emotional factors of human history. His deepened reverence for any person's real communion with the living Christ became to many a source of triumphant joy. His reborn sense of a human being's grand potential in the God-given process of regeneration found its graceful expression in a sermon he preached twice on a word which Europe's first Christian church received from St. Paul when he was in prison: "I can do all things through Christ which strengthens me."[2]

The beginning of the year 1947 was an eastern winter in Berlin. Dibelius and his ailing wife were still living in the damp basement of his native Lichterfelde. One of his sons had fallen in action, the other was reported missing in the east. The loving father never uttered any word of lament. Yet there were others to whose moanings he could not shut his ears. In that harsh and frosty winter he pointed out to the Allied liberators nine little children. These children were involved in the endless trek of the population outlawed and exiled from the area in which both Dibelius and his son had served their first years of pastoral work. The beloved stretches on and beyond the

_____

[2] Philippians 4:13.

River Oder, for centuries the most Protestant of the whole continent, were now being transmuted into a Soviet protectorate under pretext that they were a "Polish compensation area."

A well-informed British observer said that it was "monstrous that Poland, whose integrity had been guaranteed by the Allies, should be compelled to accept a loss of territory on the mere say-so of the Russians about the wishes of the population and while the war was still on."[3] He pointed out, moreover, that the western Allies "should have seen in Stalin's territorial claim a proof of bad faith, have refused to countenance such transfers until a fair expression of the people's will had shown that there was a demand for them and have pushed our troops as far east as possible. All the evidence is that the Russians, then as now, were not prepared for a head-on collision with the Americans and that they would have accepted whatever the Americans had the courage to demand. Instead we had the disastrous western compensations to Poland and the concession to communism of the iron curtain frontier which splits Europe and makes it not a viable unit. Even if we could not have prevented the Russians from occupying some Polish territory, we could have avoided the fatal blunder of underwriting Russian bad faith by recognizing the annexation."

Now the nine children who moved Dibelius' heart and spirit so profoundly came from the southern part of Poland's fateful compensation area. Their journey from Silesia to Berlin, some 200 miles, lasted two icy weeks longer than the two days actually needed even in emergency times. Their eighteen feet were blue and bloodless at journey's end. Their upper limbs and, in fact, their lives were saved by immediate amputations. This surgery could be performed only in the old capital, now slowly beginning to benefit from such medical supplies as were shipped from happier shores where Christian people had been moved with compassion.

Yes, medical help was arriving from the United States! And

---

[3] Christopher Hollis, British M.P., in a review of James P. Warburg's *Germany: Key to Peace*. London, 1954.

there were those who made a modest beginning at giving new substance to the wrecked city of four millions.

The group which was first to dig breaches in the mountainous mass of ruins was backed by a religious body which Dibelius had as yet been given little chance to contact. It was the Friends Ambulance Unit which rented a half-burnt cottage, standing close to huge Nazi barracks no longer filled by the ferocious noise of young Germans taught and trained to shrug their shoulders toward all human suffering, including their own. While the more political branches of the occupying powers were busy in exhibiting the largely unknown horrors of the now closed Nazi concentration camps, and while the Eastern elements of the victorious allies quietly abducted thousands of ex-Nazis to distant areas of isolation, here in the British sector of Berlin a veritable haven of calm security and sustaining comfort was laid out. Ruhleben Cottage was even more beneficial than could be told from its local name, Life in Rest and Reconciliation.

The leaders of the cottage group, Neville Coates and Kathleen Gough, will probably never be enrolled on an imperial honors list; yet they and their team managed to save untold numbers of waning lives. They were not only the first efficient welfare team but also the one extending material aid, at their own risk, to the churches east of Berlin right into the Soviet zone. They were quick to convert speedy jeeps and heavy trucks into conveyances for milk, cereals, sugar, dried fruit, and the badly needed bandages for young and old civilians. They offered one vehicle each to a parish for one week. Actually Dibelius and his staff obtained a Quaker driving license for ten days and he was put in a position to select whatever he wished from the treasures of canned food and of that stimulant much glorified by pre-war continental tradition, coffee unground, ground, blended, or powdered for instant use.

Always retaining his dignity, the impoverished Bishop was by no means insensitive to the tempting display of nourishment, unfamiliar as it had become to his family and staff members. In their wonted quiet efficiency, the young Quaker ladies gave him

a warm cup of cocoa before they took him to the barracks won-
derland. As they conducted the utterly silenced visitor along
the path laid out within the forest of cans and cases of all
sorts of aid material, the girls were not much surprised by his
solemn delight over this promise of food for the starving and
the invalids of his diocese. What did surprise them greatly was
the Bishop's firm request to fill the truck not with food and
bandages, but almost exclusively with stearine candles.

The time was the late fall before the second postwar winter,
which was to be more icy than the first one. The Soviets had
drastically cut down the ration of fuel, gas, and electricity to all
Berlin's civilian population. Millions of utterly disillusioned
people sat in the cold darkness. Dibelius said to the friendly
ambulance people, "If you can give us actual light and there-
with a little warmth, you will grant us more than we may expect
from others."

Neville and Kathleen promised to ask for means of lighting
at home. Most correctly, the Bishop handed back the lorry license, only to get it back when Kathleen, after a three weeks'
interlude of effectual prayer and concerted action, appeared at
his house in the American sector to break the news that the
big chocolate factories of Britain had substantiated their share
of Quaker support in "candles for homes and churches in East
and West Berlin."

In a short time thousands of families queued up in the parish halls for what they labeled, not inappropriately, Cadbury's
and Fry's and Rowntree's candles. When most private homes
had obtained their portions the Advent season arrived and a
surplus was still available. With these extra candles an ancient
eastern custom was happily revived. Four Advent carol services were held in some twenty churches during the month of
December, the Bishop preaching first in the half-demolished
Church of the Twelve Apostles. Praises and thanks were sent
up to him who once had sent his friends and disciples to bring
light to all the world.

Members of the occupation personnel walking along the
snowy streets of a city bereft of gas and electricity were over-

whelmed when they caught glimpses of almost legendary and yet quite unpretentious illumination. The ancient Advent wreath, long despised as sentimental and contrary to the hardened Nazi manliness, was hanging again in homes of every denomination! Its burning lights increased with each of the four Sundays, as the cold season brought nearer the happy return of the radiant night when God's own Son was born to overcome the works of darkness and to redeem the people of good will from all coldhearted action and devilish device.

While it is true that the Orthodox Church in Russia even in her state of captive agony (officially euphemized as state-protection), remains the Church of Easter, Protestants in Central Europe divide their attention in the Christian year between Advent and Passion Week. In theology Dibelius has often warned both pietists and intellectuals not to devaluate the cross of Christ by making it appear the only symbol worth projecting in man's effort to fill his earthly life with Christian inspiration. In Holy Scripture there is a rich and colorful variety of the "things above" which man is called to set his affection on. Here the Bishop saw the practical value of the research on ways of worship by the ecumenical Commission on Faith and Order. Here also he was able to discover some good in the much disputed liturgical reform within the Lutheran Church. For him the happiness of a Christian life has always rested with the adoration of God as man incarnate:

We should do ill to forget, in our yearly preparing for the Christmas anniversary, that the dawning of Advent is a progress to triumphant victory. It is the pilgrim's progress toward the fully assured goal of the marriage feast in heaven.

In his pursuit of the heavenly way of perfection, the Christian is not to be lured into despair by accepting all the provoking acts of his non-Christian adversaries as God-appointed stations on the road of eternal judgment.

To the Christian renewed and trained in Advent, none of the temporal phenomena are to be dramatized to the point of a final impression.

Neither death nor life, neither principalities nor powers shall be able to separate us from the love of God which is in Christ. Without his final triumph, there would be no good reason for any earnest pilgrimage, neither for holding Advent nor for honoring Good Friday.

The historical order for which Christians rightly prepare, will bring the reversal of nearly all secular evaluation. Already he has put down the mighty from their seats and exalted them of low degree. He has filled the hungry with good things.

American friends who heard the Bishop expounding the lesson of the last Sunday in Advent asked him at once to send a Christmas broadcast across the Atlantic. At the time many Americans were agitated about the Russians setting up a Soviet-German government in Pankow, thus splitting up more fatally the city to which all the Big Four had granted the right to remain a unit with international status pending the general peace treaty. The broadcast message contained these words:

Brothers and Christian friends in America, on this holy night my greetings go out to you from Berlin, the newly divided capital of Germany. Greater than all the gloomy division, however, is the wholeness of God's design for any nation. Brighter than all the darkness evolving from our human frustration is the light and the redeeming ascendancy of this holy night.

To every man with any sense of expectation the angel of God is near. Overcoming every distance, overpassing every zone of clouds and curtains, the angel says to the faithful tonight as he said to the shepherds on the meadow of Judaea: "Fear not, for behold, I bring you good tidings of great joy which shall be to all people." To all people is indeed a reassuring word for the Christians of our eastern parts. No matter how often we may have been disappointed by the mighty in war and after war, no matter how sadly we may have felt frustrated in our own fight for clarity and light, tonight we can join the humble shepherds, the unpretending and even the poor in spirit, waiting for the man born to be King to take our soul, our life, our all.

The God in whose image we were made in our beginning is the loving Father of all. Even today his family is happily composed of faithful men from many nations. His fatherly ways are ever so clear. But then they are also very consistent. Not in any zone, not in any hemisphere will he have the gates of hell prevail against his people. He has shown us the wonder of a new creation. He presents us afresh with a life to live in love and worthy aspiration.

In the same winter when Dibelius answered anxious questions of western Christians by that broadcast, the Soviet leader of "progressive women," Nina Dubrovskaja, published a state-authorized anti-Christmas article, in the *Pravda* of Leningrad:

Science has proved that Jesus Christ never existed. Christmas and other religious holidays are only exploited to distract the workers from the class struggle. Religious holidays play a reactionary and anti-social role. They disseminate an anti-scientific concept of nature and society, distract believers from the fulfilment of their production tasks, and encourage drunkenness and absenteeism from work. Religious beliefs ham-string the workers in working out the Marxist philosophy, and consequently prevent workers from becoming active full-fledged builders of communism.

To eliminate Christmas from the calendar of all progressive nations became a practical point in the program of world revolution. The sound above the ground of Bethlehem, still ringing out from the memorable company of lowly shepherds and a multitude of the heavenly host, was thus included in the "superincumbent strata of society which had to be sprung in the air," if the proletarian movement was to supersede Christendom as the majority movement of Europe and America, in accordance with the Communist Manifesto.

Dibelius would be ready to prove that his old frontier people, the hundreds of thousands of his friends now among the refugees and the displaced persons, had little in common with the spiritual tiredness of the more western European areas, little in common also with the defeatism of oriental cultures rightly evaluated by America's thinkers.

As to the Communist Manifesto, Dibelius did not deem it his calling to answer its challenge with a speedy counter-proclamation. He felt he should observe how great and how deep his afflicted country's renewal would appear to be after some years of West-supported reconstruction. He would agree with the often reiterated statement that those European nations in which clerical and feudal injustices were compounded are ever so receptive to aggressive anti-Christian propaganda. But then he also had good reason for pointing out that the encroachments recently experienced in his frontier land were not unlike the authoritarian iniquities supported by ecclesiastical rulers long before Hitler's time.

The years after Hitler's downfall were for Dibelius the "acceptable time" to prove that his borderland minority were still the people of a faith moving mountains. However cunningly the new authoritarians couched their proletarian philosophy in the language of science, he knew that the enduring concept of human life and destiny "begins and ends with presuppositions of faith" never to be reached by scientific speculation. For a Protestant of East Germany, no historical event is seen in its proper perspective in a reasoning process which leaves no room for the divine initiative, "new every morning" and ever again experienced by those concerned with ultimate values.

CHAPTER THIRTEEN

Spirit That Quickeneth

DIBELIUS would have been the last to deny that in some parts of Europe traditional church life had long deteriorated into a clerical practice, leaving the masses to seek refuge in some defeatist religion, or in superstition. In 1947 he prefaced his "Call to Prayer" with the prophecy that the majority of Europeans would be lost spiritually unless they were saved through the minority who were given to humble prayer:

The whole of Europe now depends on those who believe in the power of intercession and are determined to apply the message of Christ in new ways, awakening the social conscience within the group of those faithfully enduring in his disciples' succession.

Some of the western Allies denoted East Germany as the Junker area, thus placing it at the low level of backward colonial lands. Though Dibelius assented to the land reform which did away with the last traces of the church's vested interests, he pronounced it a fatally cheap bargain for Russia's world program to transmute Europe's most Protestant area into a mission field of the anti-Christian archpontificate. Soviet propaganda might rouse the resentment of subdued classes in

all five continents, but some ten millions of German descent
would have to be deported or liquidated before the many lovely rural towns and modest villages east of Berlin and Brandenburg would receive willingly Moscow's imposingly red-robed
pontiffs.

Unless the West made up its mind to sell out Europe, there
could be no mission field for communism as a religion in Dibelius' homeland. The land of Luther's Reformation would continue for a long time to stand out from disrupted France, fermenting Africa, and the Islamic Middle East where a decadent
feudal order was only now in the process of disintegration.
Could it be taken for granted that India, with her loose relationship in the British Commonwealth, would be able to sur-
mount the caste system without the ambiguous intervention of
Communists from the north? To compare the field of Central
and East Germany with China and Formosa would also be misleading. Prussian statism may have been rigid; yet it never
produced the injustices legalized by the Far East's traditional
bureaucracy.

By such reasoning East Berlin's bishop tried to remind American Christendom that its spiritual background was not confined to seventeenth century nonconformity, much less to Jef-
fersonian enlightenment. The great numbers of nineteenth century immigrants from Germany, Switzerland, The Netherlands,
and Scandinavia, cherished a creative memory of Wittenberg,
of Luther's Wartburg and Calvin's Geneva. Increasing numbers of American Catholics continued spiritually loyal to Eternal Rome, after all, a European city too.

A more critical observer might well ask if Dibelius should
not have been more frank and daring in his words to America.
He could have said that the American dream of evolution and
earthly perfection has graced the transatlantic Protestant tradition with some noble virtues, but that these long-respected
virtues lost something of their luster when the hemisphere became involved in a global situation in which the smiling habit
of bourgeois people could no longer express the Christian expectation. Might not Dibelius have underlined that other state-

ment of Reinhold Niebuhr—that even the constitutional monarchies of the northern and western European nations exhibit some of the wisdom inherent in the more organic forms of society, which the more rationalistic conceptions of a purely bourgeois order lack?

Aware of America's changing scene and of the challenge implied in that change, Dibelius always held to the concept of God's clear design in the course of mankind's history. Over against the anonymous and therefore unconvincing ostentation of a collective monolith, he felt sure that, after a second world war, the manifold communities of commonwealths and uniting nations would offer new scope to individual decision. He was in agreement with leading American thinkers: the God of history would not be the personal Creator and Preserver that he is, if man were not to rise up from the "baffling configuration" of our century with a personal choice of loyalty, in Europe as well as in other lands.

Dibelius had made his choice at the very beginning of our century. Never would he depart from that early decision. His loyalty belonged forever to the Church Universal, the visible fellowship of all believers, deeply rooted in history, creative and effectual as a working relationship over all the earth.

Three years after the Allied victory the universal church was still very much "in process of formation." It is true that a constitution with a promising preamble had been drafted for a World Council. But its designer, the Anglican archbishop William Temple, had died before the end of mutual aircraft bombing from which his own Lambeth residence suffered so greatly.

George Bell, the Bishop of Chichester, and some few others stepped in to incorporate the long-envisaged world fellowship of "churches which accept our Lord Jesus Christ as God and Savior." Public opinion was naturally still rather anti-German, so that neither Dibelius nor any other German was invited to attend the conferences preparing for a Christian World Assembly. It was the able and efficient Dutchman W. A. Visser t'Hooft who finally brought the various continuation committees of Stockholm, Lausanne, Edinburgh, and Utrecht to issue joint invitations to some 400 representatives of 147 churches from 44 countries to come to Amsterdam in order to constitute formally the World Council of Churches.

When the Amsterdam Assembly was in sight in the spring of 1948, there still did not exist a unified Protestant Church in Germany. Unifying the persistent "confessions" deriving their loyalty from ancient decrees of regional rulers was long overdue. With the possible exception of Bavaria, there was no postwar sign of regional traditionalism that might produce contradictory Christian loyalties. Yet there were certain groups which appeared to Dibelius somehow rather tempted to dramatize divergences. Such divergences, in his opinion, should have been treated as starting points for prayer and meditation, and not as a basis for one-sided action.

When the aging Bishop Wurm of Stuttgart asked Dibelius to take the opening service at the constituting assembly for the new church in Germany, Dibelius rightly forecast church unity of east and west. Facing the resurgence of historic confessionalism and its divergent factors such as claims of theological infallibility, he strongly appealed to the much bewildered congregations, and indeed to Protestant public opinion generally, in order to break the stubborn opposition of circles reluctant to discern the signs of the times.

Those signs were much more clearly seen by the great number of lay people who had volunteered in the interdenominational Student Christian Movement. They had come to realize that the thought-forms of the sixteenth century no longer covered the field of history, certainly not the turbulent events of the twentieth century. Nor were the exiled pastors of the now Polish occupied areas willing to have their "united Protestant congregations" cut up into outmoded divisions of a West German tradition long surmounted in the eastern testing field. They were particularly appalled at the rather exclusive handling of the Lord's Supper when they, the refugees, knocked at western sanctuaries asking for an unqualified reception in the forthright manner of steadfast frontier people.

Dibelius did not condemn the reservations set up by some

traditionalists and by church dignitaries armed with a strict theological conscience, but neither did he hesitate to state clearly what was urgently needed for the rebirth of a church in a country utterly shaken, humiliated, and divided. For the constituting assembly of Germany's church, the E.K.i.D.,[1] he drafted articles providing for full and open communion of all the three major denominations of German Protestantism. For the opening sermon, preached in Eisenach's Church of St. George on July 11, 1948, he chose his text from the 37th chapter of Ezekiel. There the prophet outlines the covenant of peace on the occasion of David's commitment to the cause of the God of Israel and to his truly universal purpose. Before the gathering of eastern and western German church leaders proceeded to renew the holy covenant at Wartburg Castle (the historic place of Luther's Bible translation), Dibelius summed up his most prophetic sermon with three program points:

1. In humility, we accept the burden of our confessional differences as laid upon us out of God's hand.
2. It is God's sole prerogative to create unity. We wait upon his hour in patience and expectancy.
3. The prophetic office of the church becomes effectual through her vision of full unity. Undaunted she shall witness to that promised gift of God.

Five weeks after the unification of east and west German Protestant churches Dibelius was able to witness to a greater unity still. The scene of that wider witness was Holland's Amsterdam. There he was, among some 300 delegates and more than 200 alternates present, the only one who had participated in the two previous gatherings inaugurating visible unity in Christ, Stockholm 1925 and Lausanne 1927.

Though his afterwar concern was very much with the new section dealing with "the church and international disorder," it was only natural that he should also give counsel to the

---

[1] E.K.i.D. stands for *Evangelische Kirche in Deutschland*, i.e., The Protestant Church in Germany.

section continuing the work on faith and order started over twenty years earlier when Charles Brent of New York and William Temple of Manchester were the coming great church's prophetic leaders. Now in Amsterdam Dibelius was deeply moved and gratified that this section presented findings truly congenial to the spirit of the prophets, that spirit which will guide us into all truth. Brent's and Temple's and also Söderblom's voices resounded in words like these:

We come from Christian churches which have for long misunderstood, ignored, and misrepresented one another; we come from lands which have often been in strife; we are all sinful men and we are heirs to the sins of our fathers.

God's redeeming activity in the world has been carried out through his calling a people to be his own chosen people. The Old Covenant was fulfilled in the New. It is our common concern for that church which draws us together, and in that concern we discover our unity in relation to her Lord and Head. Yet we would draw special attention to a difference to which, by many paths, we are constantly brought back. Historically it has been loosely described as the difference between Catholic and Protestant though we have learned to distrust any oversimple formula to describe it. The essence of our situation is that, from each side of the division, we see the Christian faith and life as a self-consistent whole, but our two conceptions of the whole are inconsistent with each other.

In recent years, it has been given to many of our fellow Christians to rediscover what it is to be a church under the cross. There they discovered new life, found the Bible as a living, contemporary book, made a good confession of their faith, and saw the church come to life in the steadfastness of thousands of humble Christians.

Christ is moving many to a more sacrificial identification with the homeless and desperate, to a more vigorous evangelism, and to a deeper theological seriousness. In various parts of the world, he is drawing long-separate Christians toward a closer approach to unity. For the courage, enterprise, and vision which inspired them, we give thanks to our one Shepherd.

The historic background for these noble words was the city which only three years before had trembled under Nazi occupation. Now this city of Amsterdam was the happy scene of a Christian nation's homage to its Christian rulers. Not far from Amsterdam was the negotiation center of the Greater Dutch Union whose Asian part was in danger of being rent asunder through the aggressive forces of both Islam and communism. Indonesia's upheaval affected the Christian minorities just as much as the turbulent rise of the Republic of India. There were in 1948 more Indian refugees and homeless people than in all Central and Western Europe together.

To many Christians of the western hemisphere these tragic facts and figures were utterly new. To Dibelius they meant a timely warning lest his defeated homeland might lose true perspective in projecting nothing but its own agony. He knew he was all the more justified in making the Assembly's section treating international disorder fall in with some of the appeals of the Confessing Church for which he had been in prison like so many of his friends, three times as we have seen.

Unanimously the Assembly adopted words recalling catacomb-like experiences:

We are profoundly concerned by evidence from many parts of the world of flagrant violations of human rights. Both individuals and groups are subjected to persecution and discrimination on the grounds of race, color, religion, culture, or political conviction.

The true church has always demanded freedom to obey God rather than men.

It is essential that the churches observe the fundamental rights in their own membership and life, thus giving to others an example of what freedom means in practice.

The churches are guilty both of indifference and of failure. While they desire more open honesty and less self-righteousness among governments and all concerned with international relations, they cannot cast a first stone or excuse themselves for complacency.

The establishment of the World Council of Churches can be made of great moment for the life of the nations. It is a living expression of a fellowship transcending race and nation, class and culture. Its aim will be to hasten international reconciliation through its own members and through the cooperation of all Christian churches and of all men of goodwill.

Before the many participants of that unprecedented assembly went back to bring the news of "our century's one great fact" to their distant communities on this or that side of the iron and bamboo curtains, Dibelius was requested to preach a farewell sermon.

A Chinese delegate said that the closing sermon preached on that first September week-end in Amsterdam's Western Kirk was a climax comparable to the event of Pentecost, and indeed he was not left alone in uttering such an appraisal. The text was taken from the passage describing how the disturbed disciples received Paul after he had been saved from his persecutors by escaping in a basket over the wall of Damascus: "Then had the churches rest throughout Judaea and Galilee and Samaria, and were edified. Walking in the fear of God and in the guidance of the Holy Spirit, they were strengthened and multiplied" (Acts 9:31).

The Holy Spirit is with us here where we commit our common future to our Lord. In the guidance of the Holy Spirit we have covenanted with one another. We have been graced with comfort and unfolding strength in the very presence of the Spirit. Its work of redeeming and gathering is an undisputed fact. And we know our faith cannot endure, if it does not live on facts, proved in history and testified over all the inhabited earth.

It is the Church Universal which is alive; the church visibly reunited, composed of the unknown and yet well known; as dying and, behold, we live; as chastened, and not killed; as sorrowful, and now rejoicing.

The covenant of our gathering here is our stay and our strength. Past and beyond the agony of strife and sad division, it is our charter. We are chartered now to go forth and multiply the seeds of the Spirit.

We have a legacy just as holy as it was with those who were promised the power of the Spirit, when they saw their Lord ascending. We, standing now in their succession, may well proclaim the fact of our century to the ends of the earth. God's spirit is here. He is with us again quickening, gathering, and comforting those in anguish, saving us all from the gates of hell.

Future records of church history will have it as an accepted fact that the preacher who had kept Christ's solid promise to Peter (Matthew 16:18, 19) as his watchword ever since he propounded "the century of the church" long before the second war, attained a lasting world renown in 1948. Eisenach and Amsterdam came as the harvest after a slow ripening, a heavenly gift to a patient husbandman.

When the husbandman came home from the Netherlands' rich harvest field, he brought with him seeds of a new life potential for the "dry and dreary sands" of his warstricken eastern provinces. The turning of that wilderness into a garden was a cultural task whose fulfilment required a strategy just as global as the undertakings of the secular agencies now lining up for winning the world-wide cold war by totalitarian methods. Though Protestantism was intrinsically averse to totalitarian trends, it could still be comprehensive.

What Berlin's bishop did on his return from Amsterdam struck many Europeans as a venture resulting from a strong awareness of the limits of the political sphere. This awareness which had dawned on most of the covenanters at the World Council's first assembly proved to be a prolific soil for an outgoing Protestant cordiality and openness. In the words of the *Christian Century's* Theodore A. Gill, such an openness and comprehensiveness might well "hasten the ecumenical day." If that ultimate day should not come too soon, it should yet not be postponed because of denominational supersensitivity or self-assertiveness. For centuries continental state-church leaders had despised the Free Churches not only because they were few in numbers, but also rather because they would not conform to the persuasive standard of a religion fully domesticated. Dibelius was glad to realize that at last the days were over when the Christian communion was a matter of social convenience. The church's call to social responsibility was no longer being divorced from the call to repentance, solidarity, and brotherhood. No longer was the kingship of Christ to be cramped by the corruptible and perishable forces including the powers that be.

Toward the end of 1948 when Berlin was still overhung by the Soviet's total blockade, Dibelius invited spokesmen of all the "little" churches to form an eastern regional council for ecumenical affairs. The invitation was accepted with unprecedented gladness. Baptists, Mennonites, Methodists, Old Catholics, Quakers, and officers of the Salvation Army came to form that regional council, under Dibelius' chairmanship. Barriers of long standing were overcome when the Bishop suggested that a Methodist superintendent, Ernst Scholz, be elected vice chairman of the council. When the Methodist spokesman then described the Bishop as their "well-trusted shepherd," the chartered freemen's applause would not end. There were fine guardians among the Free Church people too!

These shepherds watched together over an area warstricken and for a long time still to be surveyed by surly masters sending out so many hirelings. But when the true shepherds joined their hands over long-standing walls of division, they trusted in the Spirit and in the promise of its blessed fruits: joy, peace, longsuffering, gentleness, goodness, and faith.

CHAPTER FOURTEEN

Greater the Will

WHEN THE history of European integration finds its proper place in the chronicles of mankind, the year of Amsterdam will stand out as the time of three basic addresses, through which a faith strong and simple challenged the desperate diehards in the realms of self-assertive power politicians and those who habitually shut up the spirit in the hollow vessels of tradition. The man responsible for those unforgotten speeches had this to say about the way in which the divine intent would forever remain the guiding principle in the development of the nations:

The word of God is utterly different from the propaganda of men. The word is never spoken in order to advance a worldly interest. Those who proclaim it rightly gain disadvantage from it more often than not. What God's word is meant to serve is truth. And the center of truth is this: God has given his Son to this world to save men from the sinful strivings which result in world chaos.

It is one of the universal facts in history that the hearts of men are still being caught and even vanquished and turned by the word just as it happened on the first day of its proclamation. Those who have preached the word for the greater part of their lives remember grave periods of time in which they thought all their work fruitless and vain. Then suddenly some unexpected third-door neighbor comes around to tell you that ten years ago you said something which he scribbled down to keep it as a living talisman, as the profitable servant did in the parable of our Lord. Another creature, hardly known to you in person, surprises you by revealing that one short sentence of your many sermons has engendered the total change of his life.

When you hear that, you are ashamed and happy at the same time. Out of yourself, you have done nothing. You have just preached the word of God, simply and humbly. Most strangely, however, God intertwined and fully united his richly sovereign word with your poor and fragile utterings. He has made you laborers together with him.

For those who have worked with Dibelius in office, he has made it by no means easy to ascertain what yardstick he himself has come to apply to the battle of his life. His distaste for dramatizing human accomplishments, and his reluctance to make his adversities appear anything but "lack of loyalty causing him to weep with Peter," are both deep enough to win respect and warm admiration.

If God wills it that I fail and sink, no man shall lift me up. And woe to me if I ever forget how utter uncertainty and doubt brought me early near the haughty and the wicked. The Creator who says no to all wickedness and pride, has said his no also to the ecstacy of an overweening intellect.

When thus deceived and self-frustrated, what could I do but wait? Waiting can be a sober and most serious undertaking. Its very passiveness makes an instrument out of man, so that he shall no longer waste himself. Of an instrument each small function is somehow changed whenever it becomes part of a greater, an organic being. Then the time of uselessness is over. Wholesome work begins to enliven the tiniest element. Man becomes man again, however much of his godliness was depraved in the reign of rational enlightenment.

The rediscovery of the Son of man as the true brother of the

sage and of the poor in spirit alike is both a healing and a creative factor in human integration. Even to the smallest of men
a magnificent task shall be assigned, a task not envisaged as long
as the horizon was either a mirror of self and more self, or
something even more monstrous.

These words were spoken to more than 3000 young people,
who had come to Saxony's Mount St. Peter in spite of traffic
restrictions imposed on church-sponsored tours over all the
Soviet zone of Germany. The Bishop knew about the disad-
vantages which the young Christians had increasingly to under-
go. But had he ever promised a comfortable time to those who
went the way of Christ in Eastern Europe? Some of them remembered very well what he had said before the Communists
lowered their beguiling mask:

What a creditable undertaking, to swim against the violent
current! What a praiseworthy pledge, to hold the banner high
in spite of the firing at the faithful few by the encircling foes!
Here is the chance to follow Christ in the simple way of bearing his cross.

Within the fellowship of a new generation of firm and faithful followers, he recalled an even more decisive period of his
own battle against the subtle workings and glamorous offerings
of the Tempter. With a fulness of self-commitment in which
a good Methodist would greatly rejoice, Dibelius set forth to
the people gathered on the slopes of that eastern mountain how,
some fifty years earlier, he had his life's direction altered by the
searching appeal of Christ:

The learning which I impart is not my own; it comes from
him who sent me. Anyone who is prepared to do his will can
tell for himself whether such learning comes from God or
whether I am speaking on my own impulse. The man who
speaks on his own impulse seeks to win credit for himself. When
a man seeks to win credit for one who sent him, he tells the
truth; there is no dishonesty in him.[1]

---

[1] John 7:16-18.

This unreserved adoption of the mind of his divine Brother is probably the secret of his leadership. His passionate reliance on the seeking love of his Maker is nothing short of a kind of human mystery. This is deeply enshrined and yet it gleams forth, in moments of grace, through his acquired immunity to the subtleties innate in every man. It is revealed also by his sovereign dealing with the dishonesties known to Christ even in the company of his first disciples.

The man often praised for his facile display of strategic and persuasive methods of action has made the most uncompromising statements at certain turning points. He has done so with a clarity that has made the ecumenical trend a spiritual reality bordering on the commanding witness of men like John Wesley and Charles Haddan Spurgeon.

His long-standing solidarity with the Swiss-born Baptist, Jacob Meister, was proved when in reassessing the methods of foreign missions, he soberly applied to his own aspirations the words of Spurgeon:

I realized that God could save the world without me. But when he told me that I might help him, I praised him for the honor and the privilege.[2]

The "privilege" assigned to Dibelius, and indeed his shield of honor, is the unification of the church in Germany.

That sermon of mine on the unity once entrusted to David the King and gloriously set forth by God's prophet for all future time—that sermon preached in Eisenach's St. George's beneath our great Reformer's mighty fortress is the one which worked on me while I preached it; it made me understand what Christ has in mind when he expects from his disciples that faith which will move mountains.[3]

After the Wartburg wonder of a mountain-moving faith and

---

[2] Quoted in Dibelius' address at the Willingen Conference of the International Missionary Council, 1952.

[3] Extract from a press conference held with Eisenach's Soviet-controlled press representatives.

the manifestation of the Spirit's presence in Amsterdam there followed a third event: the centenary call to consider what the church had done, and what she had left undone, in saving the souls and bodies of the millions losing stability and security in a hundred years' industrial upheaval. The centenary jubilee which Dibelius attended was held in Bethel Center, the foundation of Bodelschwingh, who was for Germany what Chalmers had been for Scotland and Oberlin for Alsace and the Vosges. One-third of Bethel's facilities were still not being used, for roughly a million people had been deported to escape Hitler's gassing campaign directed against those suffering from mental disturbances. There were also traces of military destruction.

The more quiet autumn of 1948 had come. There were still some 8000 invalids. To their most receptive and expectant community, the bishop spoke these reassuring words:

Nowadays we set so many hopes on the European Defense Community. I would like to rouse your interest in a Europe united to safeguard the weak and the poor from undue punishment and from extirpation. The pressure exerted on this noble institution was unknown to many of our own nation. Nor were the western Allies sufficiently informed to save the hundreds and thousands who went to the gas camps before the Allied advance.

To make such happenings impossible for all future time, the whole of Europe should unite to restore our fathers' faith, which honors the image of God in any little one begotten of man.

Mine is not the concept of an enthusiast projecting a final war to end war. What I am interested in, as a determined follower of Christ, is the task of refounding and reforming what lies before us.

God has chosen to act in an atmosphere of freedom. What he created is meant to unfold according to his will. Only men place living creatures in iron cages, and men do this not only with animals, but also with their human neighbors destined by God to live and grow in freedom.

God erects no barbed wire. Nor does he set up frontier-posts. All that is done by men long alienated from God's shelter and protection. Let Bethel's hundred-years-old settlement then rise again to become what its Hebrew name denotes: a shelter and a house of God.

Already our British zone authorities have greatly helped to restore it, just as Americans, Swiss, and Scandinavians have contributed to other parts of our badly needed reconstruction. Let us answer them with our prayers and our thoughts, to remind ourselves as well as those in authority that a Europe without a common spiritual foundation will resemble the undertaking of the foolish man who built his house upon the sand. A united Europe will survive the floods and the winds of destruction only if it is meant to be more than an emergency operation.

If we are pledged to extend the healing spirit of Christian brotherhood, in the way in which a good family is graced in its happiness to multiply the seeds of pure and holy love, then surely the time may not be so far away when we lift up the feeble knees and make straight paths lest that which is lame be turned out of the way.

It is significant that the formation of a European community true to the genius of Chalmers, Oberlin, and Bodelschwingh was called for by Dibelius as he spoke to the very people who were frustrated by the horrors of war falsely glorified and too little repented. What he had said to the Bethel invalids in the presence of western supporters, he repeated in the Soviet-controlled suburb of Eastern Babelsberg where, in the winter of 1949, the Oberlin House was reopened as a Reconstruction Center. Here adequate employment was considered as a healing factor rather than a burden. Comradeship instead of class hatred, individual employment and proper training in a friendly home atmosphere were all to help overcome discouragement and disability among the displaced ones, the many suffering from the wounds of war and from other grave adversities.

That this wellspring of healing should attain a genuine family atmosphere was the particular concern of Mrs. Armgard Di-

belius. Her witness to the triumph of Christ in the east lives on
in such refurnished houses as Oberlin still is. In the church of
former regimes, charity had often been cold and routine. The
Bishop and his wife, however, were utterly unprofessional in
their efforts to do away with isolated institutions absorbed in
their self-sufficiency.

"Only where tenderness and true forbearance are shown on
very little occasions, only there will the great things come to
bring benefit and blessing to the multitudes for which the Lord
became our brother." Such were the characteristic words of
this brave woman, Mrs. Dibelius, to Oberlin's chief physician
before she left the Center, early and unexpectedly, to face the
prolonged endurance of her final suffering. It was in her last
Oberlin service that she heard her husband's words:

Family affection, the source of so much happiness, is never
a product of the bargaining so often used in the manipulations
of those bent on exploiting the intrinsic emotions which are
the essence of a lasting and happy partnership. Nor shall we be
good fellow workers with our Preserver if we leave the blend-
ing of our cultural legacies to the bartering busybodies who
already abuse the basic feelings of warmhearted seekers on their
sacred way toward a more lovable and more deeply enjoyable
world. The lands called Europe can be made to be our greater
home. The process will be less a matter of new creation than
of reshaping.

When missionaries, pioneers, and knights-in-order advanced
the blessings of Christ to the eastern stretches where once our
fathers tilled the soil and lately our sons surrendered their lives,
they placed linen crosses on the turrets of the strongholds in
which frail women and the native young, agonized in their conflict of loyalties, found rest and recreation. That is how the
noble banners rose over against less beneficial if more imposing
insignia of the barbarian world. With the charity of Christ,
human warmth and colors both lively and friendly came to the
uttermost parts. The blue linen cross on the white flag of Fin-
land's courageous people is still arrayed more than a thousand

miles east of where we are curtained now. The golden cross on Sweden's royal blue is another token of a common pledge beyond the national trends of modern life and action.

Are we to end the span of our whole century under a sign still utterly alien to our inheritance, so foreign indeed as the forceful emblems of world revolution have continued to appear in the eyes of loyal sons of faithfully christened fathers? To see in the cross of Christ the victorious sign of Europe's coming wholeness is more than the honoring of past tradition. A divided Europe is like an unfinished design, broken into patterns showing more and more confusion. We, however, clearly desire the moving of our continent toward and not away from the kingdom of God.

Or do you think Christ did not suffer and rise to save also the souls of those living in our century? Are we going to deceive ourselves by assuming that there are less than a tenth part[4] of loyal partners with us? Have we become victims of an enforced state-indoctrination to such an extent that lust of power and pride in man's animal capacities take the place of enriching grace and the higher human call?

Any one of our neighbors may resemble the repining wife of that nephew of Father Abraham confined to her nostalgic reveries until she was just as numbed as self-deceiving women and men are nowadays. Our Father in heaven, divine initiator of our own birthright, was not so deaf to the tenacious entreaties clamored and cried out by the earthly partner of his historic covenant. But mind you, history is a very lively process, made up of strangely living persons like you and me. If it has been said that every religion has the people who suit it, I can tell you from the world's greatest story that every continent is destined to evaluate God's revelation in that direction which the clamoring faithful have decided to take, no matter what the slogans are with the madding crowd.

---

[4] Genesis 18:23-33.

CHAPTER FIFTEEN

Over Into Macedonia

To COMPARE the warstricken areas of Western Europe with Sodom and Gomorrah was an undertaking that scandalized the proud and condescending bearers of Geneva-imported wonder drugs. Yet to him who considers how resurgent the selfishness was, and how cruel the insensibility during the postwar days, such a comparison will not seem out of place. In the address in which Dibelius made his reference to the ancient cities by the Dead Sea, he said:

We may destroy another million bodies and justify our annihilation with a philosophy run wild—yet not even the most coercive of re-educators will be able to kill the soul, the individual element shaped ever afresh by men and women through their partnership in the divine process of creation.

There is no history without the Person calling forth and guiding. History refuses to confirm the logic elaborated by those deriving all our cultural values from the exploitation of manpower. The rationalists of all the world may cast their vote against our association with the divine Initiator—we will not give up our seeking for the faithful and forbearing. We can fully rely on the covenanters' charter. There it is stated that our Preserver will not have us ravaged by brimstone and fire, not even today nor tomorrow by nuclear rain, if only our striving partners make up something like the tenth part: audible, understandable, recognizable, and lovable in the midst of the power-intoxicated nine-tenths.

At some political meetings, I have seen representatives of so-called respectable majorities who were almost mad in their outreach for added power. It was as if they could not help devouring quantities of salty water by the sea, only to leave the banquet hall with a more paralyzing thirst in their throats, so utterly sore and hoarse after a long and inconclusive arguing.

In eastern Europe they say we are soon to be silenced; our children will turn their back on us, the pilgrim people. But I leave it to you to decide if we shall conform with a world where the East and the Center are living without any personal approach to Christ as a living person, and where the West continues to indulge in its daydream of a decorative, institutional, and uncommitting quasi-religion.

Some Americans rightly detected in the Bishop's European talks after the second world war an irresistible challenge with regard to the social and cultural status of their United States. They wondered what was at the bottom of the eternal question springing up in the thoughts of the more comprehensive-minded in Germany who were really concerned about America's call, as they are still concerned about its mission to the old world.

What is most fascinating to thoughtful Germans, even if they have not wholly understood it, is the still effectual promise given by America's political founders to pledge their lives, their fortunes, and their sacred honor to a way of life that assumed a decent respect for the opinions of mankind. Honest and aspiring individuals in over-organized Europe have increasingly derived spiritual benefit from America's consistent attempt to regard history as an evolution under God, without allowing ecclesiastical authorities to exert "dominion over the faith of others."

It is in this direction that, for over thirty years, Otto Dibelius' steady counseling has centered around the unique venture called America. To him that venture does not represent democracy's last hope in the world, but rather the community of souls and bodies undaunted by coercions, and unfettered by traditions called holy but in fact merely resulting from the opinions and attitudes of earlier generations.

When, after 1945, the Bishop of Berlin made it clear to his more reactionary colleagues that the old European order with its hierarchic structure was no longer to flourish as it had for centuries, he had much of the experience of the free churches to support him. Indeed, that experience was deeply embedded within his own searching mind and charitable spirit.

When Berlin's little Moravian church celebrated the second centenary of their Czech pilgrim father's reception by the first Frederick William of Berlin and Brandenburg, the descendants of that refugee community asked Dibelius if he had not something to say by way of evaluating and restating the accepted mission of the Free Church. Dibelius answered publicly by pointing out that continuing to slight the continental free churches was incompatible with the global strategy which he, as a Christian, had been learning ever since he crossed the Atlantic. He recalled the brotherly hands stretched out by the men of America's Federal Council beneath the Statue of Liberty when first he sought a respite from the Versailles coercion and a change in the more subtle spirit of postwar Geneva. He went on to say this to the Moravian Brethren:

It has been more than a hundred years now since the profoundest elements of the Brethren's pilgrim people joined hands with devoted Lutherans and the pioneers of early English Methodism for a common great undertaking, the building of a world order with no other authority than the word of God. The joining of those hands was anything but romantic or sentimental. It took place when death was imminent to divide the sheep from the goats, the latter being the creatures frustrated in their hope to leave Europe for a better earthly living.

The scene was right in the middle of the Atlantic Ocean, a

fateful occurrence threatening shipwreck of a storeship brimful
of British and continental emigrants. With them was the devout Episcopalian who had brought new vigor to the English
church, shepherding the many with the bridle in his hand, always maintaining, "The world is my parish." Also among them
were my Lutheran and United Church predecessors, if you allow me to treat apostolic succession not too rigidly. The names
of the German churchmen in the boat were Spangenberg and
Nitschmann, and what they did was to make a whole crowd of
crew and itinerant wastrels utter their prayers and hymns and
solemn vows when ocean tempests threatened the sailing vessel most severely. Their vow was that they would never permit
their national or even their confessional divergences and doc-
trinal shadings to black out the clear common witness of undivided prayer, if only they would reach the coast, the shores
of a promised land in safety.

Now they did arrive over there, and what is more, they
brought to the America then in process of consolidation values
and virtues we in Europe might well wish to have returned in
our century. They brought the graceful experience of a solidarity with all God's children, not excepting the men of low
estate. They brought with them the certainty of Christ being
a personal saver of life much rather than an ecclesiastic whose
power depends on well-studied habits of an imposing tradition.

Of course, we are still honoring Martin Luther with a reverence deep and unfailing. No man overcame the tragic storms
of his century more miraculously than he, the greatest of all
Reformers. But with some wilder tempests blowing up in our
nuclear times, no endangered soul and, in fact, no publicly
scorned community loses any of its own importance and of its
nearness to the Master rising from his rest to rebuke the winds,
to seek and to save that which was lost. That is why I have
come to feel much more at home in your fine little boat than I
did when I was very young and rather mindful of high things.

Then, turning to the Moravian Bishop, Dibelius went on to
ask quite frankly:

How do you create this warm atmosphere of sheltered happiness and calm friendliness overwhelming everyone aboard, officers, sailors, mates, and fellow passengers? Surely your little pilgrim churches have still to teach us great things. The Lord is not divided. So we shall also not divide the little band of pilgrims for which our ship was chartered to carry us nearer to our common shores, our holy city's quiet habitations.

People of many nations have come to associate with Bishop Dibelius a grandeur which is rather rare in periods and places where little minds have the great say, mocking at every single pilgrim's regress. Americans, in their turn, have sometimes overestimated the Bishop's aptitude for shaping international order, by adorning him with a stature befitting the red carpet. One of the more serious of United States licensed dailies of Berlin once asserted that he was right to warn well-meaning western Allied personnel lest they expect too much of the official from him.

When the coming president of Federal Germany's parliament publicly revealed that the western Allies would hardly favor any German individual for the first presidential elections more than the comprehensive leader of Germany's Protestant churches, the Bishop reacted by saying something like savoring not the things that be of God but those that be of men. When he crossed the Atlantic Ocean for the second time, to attend the Toronto meetings of Inter-Church Aid and other church committees, that enterprising Episcopalian, Myron Taylor, said a historic moment would be lost if Dibelius did not see the President of the United States. Debelius replied that he felt quite uncertain of his significance in the world's timing. Yet President Truman was ever so appreciative, saying he would be happy to receive him on a second occasion also. At both encounters the talks were personal, friendly, and mutually inspiring, but much less sensational in a political sense than some of the Chicago papers preferred to intimate.

Perhaps our century is fortunate in that it has world travelers with a larger vision than we associate with diplomacy, earthbound strategy, and political proficiency. Dibelius accepted the many journeys evolving from his ever-widening office with a delight that would honor the keenest and most venturing of sailors at sea.

In the summer of 1951 Paul I, King of the Hellenes, issued gilt-edged invitations to the leading non-Roman clergy of Europe to celebrate the nineteenth centenary of St. Paul's preaching on Mars Hill. Dibelius was deeply moved to see a Christian king reverently listening to an Orthodox archbishop's reciting of the words spoken to the Athenians on the same spot in its earlier pagan setting:

God has made of one blood all nations of men to dwell on all the face of the earth. He has determined the bounds of their habitation, that they should seek the Lord and find him, as he is not far from every one of us. For in him we live and move and have our being (Acts 17:26-28).

The man who repeated Paul's words in the festival congregation consisting of royalty, clergy, and peasants from the countryside around Athens, was himself history incarnate. What was left of freedom in all the nations of Southeast Europe was the achievement of the militant faithful centered around Chatzopoulos Damaskinos. He was the appointed leader of the Greek Orthodox Church.

To be a leader of that church has always meant to be a defender of the basic liberties of man. Modern democracy, it is true, was born in Greece some centuries before Christ. But after Paul had spoken in Athens and Corinth whole generations came to believe in his Lord. With Christ, the pagan concept of democratic rights was enriched and gradually transformed. The New Testament concept is a more universal and, at the same time, a more human realization of the glorious hope proclaimed to the children of God.

In the field of secular democracy, man acts upon necessity, whether in the laws of nature or in the laws of a body politic such as the state. This came out very clearly when Damaskinos and Dibelius had a personal meeting to discuss the impact of

St. Paul's Mars Hill address on ancient and modern democracy. The Archbishop of Athens had much to say to this:

It was the mission of the early church to usher in man's victory over all the deceptive illusions which enslave man through relieving him of his personal responsibilities. When the ancient Greeks, especially the slaves among them, heard the apostles of Christ give glory to the new creation, they were glad to realize the meaning of the great event which compels the animal-like evolution to break and pause and wait for a new breath to breathe into earthly vessels the breath of life. It was through Christ the New Man that the course of nature was superseded. It was through the New Man calling for successors, that those who responded found themselves becoming infinitely more than mere individuals. Their very acts of responding recreated their godly image.

Responsibility for the neighbor under God was no longer a burden imposed by the ruling deities of heathen animism. Responsibility for the fellow-New-Man became a happy sharing of Christians risen to the sacramental fulness of all given life. No bodily exertion, no political phenomenon was left any longer to anonymous functionaries of an imperial combine. Every act of the New Man's earthly existence was an item for the Book of Life. But so was every act of political suppression. And the Book of Life is being written until the last day.

Where the church has retained a loving care for man on earth, there she cannot leave unchecked the forces which hinder him from living up to the image so lovingly restored by Christ.

We in the mission field of St. Paul have had more than once to reaffirm man's sacred responsibility with Christ. The saints of our church have been the cloud of witnesses of the greatest historical fact of all times: The old order, man's history without God, and the rigid rule of the anonymous, is defeated by the humble birth and holy baptism of each little child. For the children of God are born to be free. Each birth now is the beginning of an unrepeatable personality destined to survive with his or her unique intent.

The religion of Islam has often underrated this supernal near-ness of each man to his Father. Just as Islam, our neighbor con-tinent's religion and philosophy, does not fully evaluate the sacramental character of a man's and a woman's most personal relations, so also it is apt to submerge the weaker nations, un-dercutting their spiritual and cultural identity. Outwardly our Greek nation has always been weaker than the Arabs and the Turks. But with us has often been the miraculous strength of Christ and his saints.

If you look around, you will see quite a few of my neighbors wearing medals with only two dates: 1453 and 1828. It is the honored emblem of the families whose members took part in the resistance movement. The two years on that medal mark the reascendance of the Christian kingdom of Greece over against the barbarian empires of the Turks and the Arabs.

Yet the struggle for personal and political liberty goes on. Just as the British, in a holy alliance, helped us in 1828, they and the Americans came to our rescue also when German Nazis made our king and government flee to the south of Africa. Then again our church stepped in to safeguard cultural and political continuity. She is still safeguarding at this time when all our European neighbors are under atheist communist rule.

When I was appointed Regent of all Greece I helped to re-store our king, because after all his suffering, he was the em-bodiment of the final victory to be won by every God-inspired person over the soulless monolith of material power.

Would not a full reunion of northern Protestantism with that Athenian kind of Orthodoxy bring much good to the whole of Europe? With Athens' spiritual leader Dibelius felt that the people and the very soil of the Mediterranean and Agaean shores had retained something of the elementary virtue of the gospel entrusted to them by Christ and the apostles. Here, at the place where Europeans first heard the holy name of Jesus Christ, he had a heightened sense of the mystical and euchar-istic quality of the hallowed parts of the earth.

Like an expectant pilgrim Dibelius proceeded to trace the

narrow path which Paul ascended from Cavala on the coast of
Macedonia up to Philippi where Lydia, the seller of purple, was
the first one in Europe to receive the sacrament of Jesus. A period of nineteen centuries had passed by. An East German disciple, laden with much of Europe's changing history, quietly
wandered over the slopes of southern Macedonia, soon to find
himself reliving the vision which appeared to Paul when he was
still at work in Asia. The vision was Europe's destiny, her irre-
vocable voice: "Come over into Macedonia and help us!"
(Acts 16:9)

Dibelius heard that voice entreating him just as fervently
when, a week after his quiet Philippian pilgrimage, he found
himself in a congregation of some 400,000 Christians of Central and East Germany. They had rallied to the international
city of Berlin for five days in order to witness to the endurance
of the faithful in regions of Europe where the word of God and
baptism in the name of Jesus Christ were considered as unwel-
come as they had been to the pagan mighty of ancient Greece
and Macedonia. This was the lay people's Kirchentag, an encounter of east and west with a strong emphasis on eastern
Christians communicating both their trials and their opportunities, their setbacks and their new approaches conditioned
by the Soviet monolith's crushing of many valued traditions.

During those five days, the gray clouds of an eastern totalitarian climate were pierced by a brightness of the spirit, by an
evangelistic drive capturing even the city's Soviet sector. Drivers
of Communist propaganda lorries went into hiding as if their
motors could not stand the triumphant sound of hymns and
Bible slogans re-echoed from the heavily trodden roads, from the
crowded streetcars and metropolitan trains, from the innumerable soapboxes on which priests and laymen proclaimed the
risen Christ as their uniting bond:

*Though some of the foreign powers may continue to advo-
cate our land's partition—though we may have forfeited our
former function as a factor in the making of world history—
what is now the Christian minority of our country finds itself*

*blessed with an unexpected growth in inward strength through
new kinds of person-to-person encounter.*

*Though political party slogans may continue to poison the
air, yet we are brothers, and in Christ our fellowship is one.*

Dibelius saw to it that the Kirchentag, which was soon to advance further east to Leipzig, a city 100 per cent in Soviet
hands, should not become an official institution. He knew anything officially organized was bound to invite state interference. It was just this wise refraining from state-connection
which made the subsequent rallies of the lay people great suc-
cesses in the eyes of east and west alike.

With the mobilized spiritual forces of almost half a million
active Christians strongly behind the witness of his church, Dibelius was in a position to approach the Big Four powers of the
world as they endlessly discussed how parliamentary elections
could be carried out in a country cruelly curtained and now in
the process of interzonal self-annihilation. The suggestion of
the Bishop and his council was this:

*That the High Commissioners entrusted with the govern-
ment of our country may make provisions for the preparing,
safeguarding, and controlling of equal and democratic elections
in all four zones of Germany and in the international city of
Berlin through the United Nations organization. If that organization is not in a position to procure neutral controllers in
sufficient number and equipment, the regional and local coun-
cils of the church will name and offer disinterested Christian
men of blameless record to safeguard the proper functioning of
Germany's first act of democracy, in every town and village.*

American and British chief advisers were much in favor of
the Bishop's noble if unexpected suggestion. The records of
Germany's Control Commission will some day reveal which of
the occupying partners are most responsible for the rejecting of
the offer and for the continual postponement of nation-wide
elections, without which all the brilliant talk of the hope and
wonder of democracy is hardly more than sounding brass in
the ears of the long-frustrated millions in Martin Luther's land.

CHAPTER SIXTEEN

Inroads of Independence

EACH NATION has its reformers. Each nation has also the bearers and makers of history, though they are destined to remain anonymous, or their names have attained the honor of which Christ once said it is often denied to the greatest in his own country and in his own house. If the name of Dibelius has a strangely magic sound in the ears of many eastern Europeans, it is also not surprising that such a name should be less and less identified with the resurgence of the old world in a purely western setting. His biblical approach to the life and destiny of man has been the same in his postwar office as it was when he was a rebellious leader of the young in the earlier state-church years.

With some sorrow he noticed that the amazing outward recovery of Western Germany was not matched by an increase of sacrificial love and charity toward the Christians of the East. Was history to repeat itself and prove to the world that in the subdued Protestant parts of Germany charity and love were more intensely lasting than in the florid stretches along the Rhine where once the Emperors of Rome had founded a tradition of grandeur and earthly glory?

The history of Europe, East and West, is essentially the moving life-story of her cultural and spiritual leaders. On the hinges of their words and deeds turn the events that are worth recalling, reliving, and rethinking. Significant trends will converge at certain periods. One such period was the year 1952. The failure of all-German elections was making it appear that the fate of the two Germanies for another decade had been determined. It was at this very time that church leaders of various countries joined many missionaries from Asia, Australia, and Africa in their first intercontinental meeting to reassess the methods of presenting the message in a non-Christian world. They came together at the invitation of Germany's Foreign Mission Board.

The International Missionary Council met in the lovely valley of western Willingen. The Bishop of Berlin marked the opening service with one of his favorite challenges taken from St. Paul (1 Corinthians 3:9). Here the oneness of the pilgrim people was made manifest. There was a disregard of artificial demarcations that indicated a pilgrim's progress historic in the highest sense.

Students of modern church history have remarked that some Lutherans are rather unlike Luther. Bishop Dibelius observed more than once that people calling themselves emphatically Christians are utterly unlike Christ. To the gathering of those responsible for the advancement of light he had to speak words like these:

It is not the fault of the heathen that the gospel of Christ does not get through the world more quickly and more powerfully. It is much more the fault of the Christians who, by their lives, have made Christianity difficult to believe in. In the last ten years, God's almighty arm has humbled us. All movements which have with pride and self-confidence proclaimed, We shall succeed—have failed. The church would do well to realize that failure. The church should call men out of all self-righteousness to humility. We are all under God's righteous judgment now.

Yet the time we live in is a time of great events. In such a time we need a larger vision of what God is doing with mankind. The faith of Christian men should envisage the greatness of God's action in its true proportion. As a result of his mighty grace, he calls us to his side: *You are laborers together with me.*

Dibelius had just closed the intercommunion service after that sermon on a Willingen valley's midsummer eve, when an ancient-looking parchment was put in his hands. It had been sealed by a conspicuous figure in the Soviet Union. A wonderful dream seemed to come true. The seal was that of Alexej, Patriarch of the Moscovites and of all the Russians. Could Dibelius, the letter said, come to Moscow in November, giving counsel and inquiring into the status of inner Russia's Orthodox Christians?

The Bishop of Berlin's reply was at once a positive expression of interest and appreciation. Not that he ever allowed himself to be carried away by illusions. Peaceful coexistence, however fashionable it was at that time, seemed to him a paradox where the value of individual man was distorted by materialistic concepts in two equally extreme and equally fatal directions. But there were men baptized in the name of Christ on both sides of the curtain. With a vigor seldom seen in a man of biblical age, he set out to study the traditions, laws, and usages of the church bearing the imposing title *Orthodox*, which means unfailing in righteousness and faith.

There was seldom such a time of hope and expectation as there was in the fall of 1952 A.D. The Faith and Order group of the World Council of Churches was holding a fruitful convention at Lund in Lutheran Sweden. The major denominations of the United States had recently announced a program of united service through the National Council of Churches of Christ. Deadlocks and many self-frustrations of the pilgrim people of the world seemed to be surmounted at last. Had the prayers of the righteous been so genuine and fervent that their effectiveness now became evident in history through a oneness in Christ? This oneness would be the goal of pilgrims from many lands. The end would come, and Christ, the coming

Lord of all history, was to supersede the disunity of allegedly Christian and reputedly non-Christian nations.

To the Protestants in the heart of Europe, it was no happy surprise when America's news magazine *Time* rushed forward with one of its more capricious jumps by showing the Bishop's photograph underlined, "The man who made the Patriarch ill." He had written no negative word to the Patriarch's office. He had failed to perform but one service to the High-Priest's mundane advisers; he had not rejected a long-standing and long-published suggestion from his old American friends to say or to write a word of good will to their National Council's second assembly scheduled for the same historic month of November 1952.

Granted that the journalists' statement was only indirectly true and Berlin's Bishop did not make Moscow's Patriarch really ill, it was nevertheless a meaningful incident that the Patriarch's political advisers should consider Dibelius' comprehensiveness in accepting invitations from two antipodal camps too large an amount of actual coexistence. Moscow's invitation to Dibelius was formally canceled for reasons of ill health. Nor was it renewed when the allegedly sick Patriarch rushed from one communist peace congress to another.

There was no cheer in that month of waning light. Death had come too early to Otto Dibelius' true companion. She was laid to rest in the forest burial ground within the quiet precincts of his native Lichterfelde. In that service it became triumphantly clear that neither death nor life could destroy their common life-commitment, their fellow-pilgrims' communion in Christ.

Clouds descended and enwrapped an open grave as the many hundreds were paying tributes of homage, passing by and uttering their prayers in the very ancient eastern German fashion. It was Advent in the unchanging round of the Christian year. A carol was attuned by an unseen choir, unpretentious and almost ethereal. Soon the host of mourners joined in a hymn of Advent ringing out from the wintry fog, rising to the radiant light of resurrection, expressing an exultant quietude. On his lonely way back from the graveyard Dibelius resolved to re-

sume the lowly pilgrim path, that road where the landmarks of
peace in righteousness are the only signs of promise.

After a solitary flight he arrived in Colorado's city of Denver to express his heartfelt wishes for the prospering of America's Churches of Christ "united in faith and action" at the
end of that historically significant month. He was still too
deeply moved to present long speeches. But no one who was
a witness of that Advent gathering can ever forget how Bishop
Henry Knox Sherrill welcomed Otto Dibelius both as a pilgrim and as a herald watching for the dawning of eternal day.

The pilgrim's calm independence from our earthly life's per-
plexing configuration stood out as he overcame the temptation
to seek a wailing wall. It was not within the design of following Christ that he should dwell on his personal involvements
in the events of that surprising year. He thought it was his
calling rather to draw the attention of America's churches to
other victims of Europe's unrest.

The victims whose wintry exodus Dibelius deemed worthy to
commend for prayerful intercession were a stream of eastern
migrants, more than 100,000 each year. In Denver he said these
words on their behalf:

An uninterrupted flow of people streams daily from the Soviet
east to the west. Efforts are made to discourage them from coming over. Passports which they need for crossing the curtain
line are refused to them. Those who cross the border illegally
run the risk of being shot. The only way still open is the way
via Berlin and the airlift from Berlin. Each day some 500 persons register at the West Berlin refugee reception office. Sixty
per cent of those registered are flown over to West Germany.

All our refugees arrive nearly destitute. A small suitcase is all
they have. If not all members of a family can flee, then the refugees have to reckon with serious reprisals being visited on the
relatives at home. The loss of manpower is a crime also liable
to punishment in the totalitarian state.

However, what is most oppressing to the people of East Germany is not their physical need, great as it may be especially

when sickness occurs and there are no medicines easily procurable. What causes the most serious oppression is the legal insecurity and the forcible propagation of a materialistic concept of life.

No inhabitant of the East Zone is free from the fear of sudden arrest and complete isolation in secret camps. A totalitarian system can be maintained only by secret methods of pressure.

The security of the state requires the constant practice of terrorism against all who may in any way oppose the ruling class. As soon as the rulers sense a hint of opposition to its goals and its propaganda, it acts ruthlessly. Penalties are unbelievably severe. There is no hesitation in sentencing young people of sixteen or eighteen years to twenty-five years' imprisonment for misdemeanors which, in a democratic state, would carry but a small penalty.

Since the state can never be wrong, a scapegoat has to be found whenever something turns out badly. If the Five-Year-Plan somewhere does not function, it is never the system which is declared to be at fault. Sabotage is said to have been committed and somebody must bleed for that. There is no redress against the judgment of a totalitarian state. The judge is no judge, but a public prosecutor. Whoever comes before the court will be sentenced. Right is what is useful to the state. Man's duty consists of serving social progress for the proletarian class.

Such is the quintessence of the materialistic doctrine. Its propagation begins with the smallest children in kindergarten. They learn of the Five-Year-Plan, of Stalin, the loving Father of all children in the world. Everything that recalls the words of Christ is being eliminated. To sing a hymn is an action hostile to the state. At school it goes on. True, the church has received permission to give religious instruction. But the hours allocated for that instruction are late in the day and most impracticable. A Young Pioneer, that is, a member of the State Youth Organization, is on pioneer duty on Sunday mornings. To go to church is not forbidden, but it is made impossible. Sunday is the main day for state and party action.

It must have seemed a miracle even to the Bishop himself that with all these indirect methods of pressure, there should persevere a Christian fellowship of young people at all. The fact was that it did not only endure but also grew, both in numbers and in inward strength.

Youth in Europe is always rallying to points of venture where nothing goes any longer without arguing. And Christianity was just the factor which did not "go" any longer. It did not function with any of that social backing which had been so customary in the regions of authoritarian rulers.

The shortage of pastors was already drastic. So what the young people did was to assemble, in many groups, in distant forest corners during the spring and the summer; while in wintertime they met in private apartments, so that the number limit of permitted assemblages was not willingly transgressed.

Not even the little groups, however, were conceivable to the Communist rulers in other than political categories. The individuals who followed Stalin's outlines for furthering revolution, were the sons and grandsons of the very nineteenth century people who had seen the Church of Christ as it appeared in its fatal era of statist splendor. It was most surprising that there should have emerged from deeper fountains a church concerned with man, and more especially with anyone of low estate. The secularized progeny of the earlier Marxists had always distrusted the well-to-do who went to Bible classes. So it was obviously horrifying to observe how interesting and uplifting life with Christ, the word in action, had seemingly become.

When, in February, 1953, more than forty young leaders were arrested, Dibelius wrote to their elders and supporters:

The enemies of Christ have always thought to apply their style of methods by sparing bishops and others in prominent positions when they hit out at those who labor unto the harvest. The method of Christ, however, is atonement accomplished through common loyalty. Christ's strength found its full scope in the weakness of Europe's first apostle. Now his strength is made perfect in the cells of Rummelsberg, Waldheim, Bautzen, and Torgau. As the warders of those camps and prisons have been made instruments of openly declared deniers of Christ, we may well rise to proclaim:

"Our young Christian people, the Junge Gemeinde, are most worthy in our hearts, as they are precious in the eyes of the Lord."

Among the young prisoners of 1953, there was the Bishop's assistant of St. Mary's in East Berlin. He was treated by sundry methods to induce him to make a report that could be used in the show trial already framed for the Bishop. At the curate of St. Mary's and at several more of the Bishop's junior staff, identical inquiries were thrust in nightly hearings lasting from two to four hours, for almost seven months in that year. The routine of reiterated interrogations went like this:

Investigator: What is the Constitution and what are the rules of the Protestant Youth organization?

Interrogated Pastor: The youth groups of our church have no constitution. Nor have they rules beyond the parish level. They are only parts of the respective parishes.

Investigator: We have counter-evidence that the movement of *Junge Gemeinde* has been organized to break the monopoly of the eastern Youth Pioneers, and that several staff members of Dibelius have taken a leading part in that illegal counter-organization. Why is it that several youth group leaders have been trained in foreign countries?

I. P.: The Church of Christ is an international unit. The World Council of Churches is an official body of international standing. Invitations to visit other member churches are gladly accepted, as they further the contacts across zonal and national boundaries. However, one could not call that a regular training abroad.

Investigator: For what purposes is the World Council of Churches being used by Dibelius?

I. P.: The World Council is a fellowship of various church denominations holding the conviction that all true dis-

ciples of Christ are essentially one in their Lord and de-
siring to reassess that fundamental unity in faith and action.

Investigator: What action of the World Council is other than
hostile to the welfare state of the working population and
the proletarian class?

I. P.: The World Council does not spread hatred but desires
to remove artificial barriers, most of all those of misun-
derstanding and misconstruing one another.

Investigator: We have counter-evidence that the World Council of Churches is an American-supported agency for furth-
ing the political prestige of the West. Would you be ready
to sign a statement to that effect?

I. P.: All member churches contribute to the offices of the
World Council. The World Council does not serve political purposes. But it is a regrettable fact that some great
eastern churches have rejected the invitation to become
member churches of the World Council.

Investigator: That is hardly to be regretted, since the churches
of the eastern hemisphere have done well to preserve their
liberty in faith and action. You are now requested to ex-
plain how it is that the atmosphere of the World Council has been exclusively western from its very beginning.

I. P.: The documents of the World Council's First Assembly
held in Amsterdam show that that is not the fact.

Investigator: In the coming court trial, you will be given proof
of the fact that the movement called ecumenical has become a dangerous tool of American policy. Why is it that
only English is spoken at the meetings of the World Council, even in Switzerland or in the Scandinavian countries?

I. P.: German and French are also official conference languages
in the World Council of Churches.

Investigator: How is it that Dibelius so often speaks English
at his private residence? Learning English was never a part
of the education in German theological seminaries. Who
then has taught Dibelius recently?

I. P.: The Bishop's brother was one of the greatest professors

of English literature in all Germany. Both Dibelius brothers received part of their college education in Britain.

Investigator: What German documents have been translated
into English at Dibelius' private residence?

I. P.: Two sermons have been translated, one for an ecumenical service held in Berlin, the other for a church magazine in the United States.

Investigator: That is not the whole truth. We have evidence
here that the whole program of East German youth activities was translated for circulation in the British and United
States elements of the Allied Control Commission. What
amount in United States dollars did you receive for the documentation and information produced in the English
language?

I. P.: Not one dollar was received.

Investigator: You will be given a chance to revoke that statement when you stand as one of the main witnesses against
Dibelius in the public trial. You will have sufficient time
to prepare yourself for that testimony. We already have
counter-evidence that all the political and military information forwarded through Dibelius' East German staff, was
richly paid for by dollar grants-in-aid. Meanwhile you are
advised to give a more truthful answer to the following
question. Whenever Dibelius received political leaders of
Western Germany, which person of his staff was present
with him?

I. P.: I cannot answer that question directly, since I only know
of western churchmen being received by our bishop in the
same manner as he received churchmen of the east.

Investigator: You will come to regret that statement of yours,
since we have ascertained that Dibelius promised to officers of the United States High Commission not to receive East German visitors without some western agent
being present with him too. You are requested to express
your views on that arrangement.

I. P.: With your permission, I express my full doubt. The
Bishop of Berlin respects duly the Four Powers' authority.

But he can never go so far as to make the church dependent on any political power.

The investigators, four of them in the year 1953, found no end in reiterating these and other questions, directed in the same routine order to several young pastors and laymen also. They were well trained in the dialectical method. Yet they were unable to understand the structure and witness of the church. Moreover, they had the most contradictory views and impressions of America. Their evaluation of the American mind was as unrealistic as it was negative in purpose. The Marx-inspired investigators could hardly believe their interrogated victims when they pointed out how uncongenial it would be to the American concept, if an American state official accepted binding promises from a religious leader, or from any religious body.

It is true that none of the long-imprisoned young Christians could deny that public opinion in America had shown an increasing concern for Dibelius' utterings and actions in the international setup of Berlin. However, the interest which Dibelius had himself found across the Atlantic Ocean was essentially the interest of Christian individuals who realized that here was a man thoroughly determined to apply to every act of international policy a clear and consistent ethic with the ultimate sanctions of both human salvation and earthly damnation behind it.

CHAPTER SEVENTEEN

Discord and Solidarity

THIRTY YEARS of war and revolution had shaken the pattern of mankind's existence both in the old world and in the western hemisphere. Small was the number of persons who did not inwardly change through the years of outward decline.

National delegates to Denver and the true-hearted people of Gettysburg who listened to the man from Berlin after an interval of twenty-one years were gratified to realize that this was the same Otto Dibelius whose challenging proclamations they had heard at the beginning of the movement for intercultural Christian cooperation early in the century when he had vitalized a synod in Ohio. What was earlier envisaged with a fine prophetic feeling was now fully and gravely evaluated amidst the ruins of a divided continent.

"See that you be not troubled. For all these things must come to pass. But the end is not yet" (Matthew 24:6). On this command of Christ Dibelius preached on Trinity Sunday 1953 when over fifty pastors of his province were still in jail for unpublished reasons and without proper trials.

M. A. Suslov, General Secretary of the Soviet Union's Communist Party, was in Berlin at about the same time. In his presence one of East Germany's political bosses made the public pronouncement that Dibelius, with his continued requests for open trials of the arrested clergy, was not taken any more seriously than a "crying contortioner in an ill-staged melodrama."

However, the Bishop whose friends and followers were isolated from him and from their churches preferred the quiet venture of faith and patience to the blatant response of hatred, scorn, and indignation. In that Trinity sermon, he said he was learning to measure the often changing pattern of life by the Beatitudes, by Christ's proclamation of the lasting values of human existence:

For me and, what is much more meaningful today, for those in prison, the end is not yet. Wherever we find ourselves, we have to live and suffer with Christ before we are redeemed to rise and rejoice with him over the past having run its full sweep of hours. The quiet day of exultation will then be ours.

> *Until it comes in full, we wait in patience,*
> *standing in faithful expectation.*
> *Through all the night we watch,*
> *our hearts thy throne adorning,*
> *Until in clarity thy light, thy day is dawning.*

For the sake of the young pastors and student leaders kept for months in complete underground isolation, Bishop Bell of Chichester had written letters to the London Times and to the Soviet High Commissioner in Berlin. As chairman of the World Council of Churches' Executive Committee, Bishop Bell had pointed out that it was contradictory to the Charter on Human Rights, signed by United Nations representatives of the Soviet Union, to keep political prisoners in isolation for such a long time. That the powers responsible for those measures were rather slow to react to the ecumenical church's communication did not surprise those who could recall how weak and unecumenical the churches' witness was when, in the twenties and thirties, thousands of eastern Orthodox priests were liquidated without any proper trial. With that sad record in mind, Dibelius rose to the conviction that the confusion of competing forces which was now the fate of Europe could be replaced by

a new order, only if that order was the spiritual and moral issue of the new and poignant Macedonian call which he had
heard anew in Athens and on the hills of Macedonia:

> Our response to the renewed call to Christian wholeness shall
> not be delayed, even if church unity has come to be considered
> an unusual and, to some observers, even an unwelcome sign of
> Christian integration.

What seemed so unusual to the mighty of this world and em-
barrassing at least to one element of the Four Big Powers was
just that Christ-inspired attitude of world-wide solidarity.

In traditional Europe statesmen and politicians of all countries were accustomed to finding ecclesiastical allies willing to
perform the act of Judas whenever it was requested in the interest of the state machinery. In 1953 Dibelius' warning was
still concerned much more with repeated acts of betrayal inside the national church community than with indignities inflicted on the young disciples from outside:

> A church which does not associate with the cross of Christ
> the readiness to suffer in his following does not deserve to be
> called Christian. Perhaps we ought to be more careful in using
> that word. For is it not a tragic fact that Christians have be-
> come essentially lesser and weaker than Christ has been on
> earth? Are we not still surrounded by very conventional Chris-
> tians tempted to fall back into rather ossified methods of di-
> plomacy in their relations with the groups they like to call au-
> tonomous and neutral? The end is not yet, but it will come.
> And in the final battle between Christ and Antichrist, there
> will be left little scope for autonomy. There is this element of
> truth in the philosophy of world revolution, that the neutral
> camps will be overrun completely. As it is true that the Anti-
> christ claims totality, so God is not neutral either. The whole-
> ness of God does not allow truth to be divided. Christ is not
> divided. And so his church must not be divided, neither dis-
> integrated through binding loyalties of confession nor divided
> between the powers of East and West.

While Dibelius never conceals his personal affiliation with the culture of the West, while he gladly continues to cherish and honor his Lutheran background in the ecumenical body of the church, he no longer permits either East or West to impress him with exaggerated emphases on complementary truths. His insight into time's limitations has become so deep that he greatly appreciates the Greek and Russian Orthodox churches' awareness of eternity, their deeply human sense of mystery, their freedom from the pretensions and compromises of collective morality.

When the disillusioned workers of all East German cities began to cry havoc and rose to the fierce riots of June 17, it was surely more than a coincidence that he witnessed the march of the workers right in the middle of Berlin's Soviet sector. Full of sympathy and understanding, he seemed to fear no act of reprisal when he watched the brave procession outside the Foreign Mission Center near Stalin Avenue, the Eastern sector's greatest road. Not that he or any of his followers had preached rebellion. What had come to the ears of the frustrated working-class population was nothing more, and nothing less, than the words of the 99th Psalm which he had read emphatically before preaching that Trinity sermon in St. Mary's, the Protestant cathedral of the Soviet sector of Berlin:

> Thou executest judgment and righteousness,
>   thou dost establish equity.
> In thy house, the man that is strong
>   also loves righteousness.

When the Russian Red Army had forcefully suppressed the riots in that memorable mid-June week, two historical facts remained of paramount importance: the German Communists were unreliable and quite unable to control the workers in all the eastern cities; and the leaders of the Protestant churches had won the confidence of the working class through their sympathy and their identification with the workers facing exploitation and unjustifiable retribution.

Most of the active June rioters were sentenced to long prison penalties. Many of their supporters, however, found shelter and counsel in the ever-growing laymen's centers of the Lutheran and the United churches of East Germany. When Dibelius had returned from Macedonia in 1951, he found great numbers of laymen waiting for East and West Berlin's big Kirchentag.

Two years later, just after the June riots of 1953 had brought endless acts of retaliation, a still larger rally was held in the wholly Eastern city of Leipzig. Some 500,000 people went to Holy Communion in the open air and heard Dibelius giving out the watchword for another year of endurance and persever-ance, "Cast not away your confidence, since it has great recom-pense of reward" (Hebrews 10:35).

In the unrest of the postwar years, the Kirchentag rallies ac-quired a special kind of fruitful permanence though they never became part of the official church organization. Being the re-sult of independent laymen's work, the biennial nation-wide rallies and the local working groups, social, political, and vo-cational, came to fulfil the function of a stimulant and a cor-rective for the churches which, on their part, were either ex-alted or burdened by the impact of their traditions, investments, and formal institutions. Personal encounters are often easier and happier outside traditional turrets and citadels.

For all the different people meeting at Kirchentag groups and rallies, the church remained the living mother, shepherd-ing, waiting, and interceding. Perhaps she could not move and change so quickly as independent lay people could and gladly would. Yet the great living mother knew how she would bene-fit from her active and sturdy children, as any mother true to her divine calling would know. Experiments in open commun-ion, joint intercession, and new ways of worship were not so heretical as they might have seemed to some ecclesiastics within their august and stately sanctuaries.

The watchword which Dibelius proclaimed on the last day of the Leipzig rally was soon to begin to work among the masses still made up of nominal Christians. The greater part of them had lost contact with the institutional churches and were about to cast away their earthly hope and trust because in their sep-

aration from the communion and life of the church they could
see no just reward for their struggling. Moreover, they had to
put up with mockery, malice, and chicanery, the ultimate weapons of the agents who guide man in a direction contrary to that
of Christ.

On leaving the mass meeting of Leipzig, Dibelius much regretted that he could not hear the manifold reaction to his restating of the apostle's plea not to "cast away." He had to go
straight from the city of East Saxony to a place which the stern
Calvinist Karl Barth preferred to keep out of his itinerary because it was situated "too far behind the golden curtain of the
West." That was Chicago's northern suburb Evanston, and the
occasion there was the Second Assembly of the World Council.
Dibelius had belonged to the Central Committee of that
Council since its first and constituting assembly held during
1948 in Holland's biggest city. Some of the unchanging critics
of the ecumenical movement, still very audible on the side of
the more rigid confessionalists, expressed a strange farewell on
the eve of Dibelius' departure from the east. He did not know
if he should take this greeting as being really funny; it sounded
thus: "Across the Atlantic Ocean, we wish you would not be
led into eternal Amsterdamnation."

Whatever the fears of some traditional ecclesiastics were
with regard to the widening premises of the church, Dibelius
was looking forward immensely to the prospect of a reunion
with his American friends and allies. He had his friends in quite
a number of different denominations. In Amsterdam he had
witnessed deeds of the Spirit. Lutherans, Methodists, Episco-
palians, Presbyterians, United and many other church people
had gladly promised to stay together in prayer and action.

Coming to America the traveler from Leipzig was eager to
look into the New York office of the National Council's Commission on International Affairs which had grown so considerably under the joint care of leading Lutherans and Presbyterians. He was sure to find in that commission a place where
the problems of the more and more divided Germany would
find an assessment dispassionate and meaningful at the same

time. In all humility, he felt he was inwardly independent enough to accept a personal invitation to see John Foster Dulles. Now the Secretary of State, Dulles had previously been the chairman of the Federal Council's Department of International Justice. Dibelius recalled how clearly the unofficial Dulles had spoken in 1948, during the Soviet blockade of Berlin, on "God's Design and Men's International Disorder."

The bishop of the long-blockaded German capital approached Evanston's Northwestern University campus with a view to witnessing the great assembly as the second test of the vitality and spiritual reality of the movement which stood for manifest unity over all the inhabited earth. For the world's tensions, by no means less tremendous in 1954 than they were in 1948, he had no ready-made solutions in his pocket. Yet while he was in America, he was eager to discover how the findings of such great conventions as Toronto and Denver had developed and how deeply they affected the policy-making forces in the United States. Would Americans and Canadians still give credence to the idea that their countries were immune to revolution? Some good professors and seminary students had honestly tried to give him that impression when they conferred a degree on him in Gettysburg, just eighteen months earlier.

With a number of more disillusioned Europeans, Dibelius had perhaps one feeling in common; he wondered if a second World Assembly could ever attain the creative stature of the first. He, for one, would ever recall and most feelingly present the great fusion of Lutherans, Calvinists, Unionists, and some smaller Free Church units into the one Protestant Church in Germany, as being the unmerited gift on the eve of the First Assembly of World Christendom. Would there now be in other home countries similar warnings and diffident utterings as he had heard when he stopped in Western Germany on his way from Eastern Leipzig to America? How many delegates would, after leaving their home country, rise to the ecumenical situation and place their responsibility to God in Christ and to the whole of human brotherhood above their national and denominational loyalty?

Would Evanston be blessed as a conference from which he could bring home to the traditional-minded this lesson, that the best of Europe was not only and not even mainly in the past? Would Europe believe and fully realize that the rediscovery of the Universal Church meant a blessing for all and a full blast into the ancient framework of tradition and self-righteousness? Would the ecumenical event of 1954 be universal and real, so that his peoples in the old world could perceive God's will, the same for any continent and nation, no matter whether old or new within the timing where a thousand years are but one day? Would the old world then come to accept the great design for all God's children, to blossom afresh and, as a new creation, to move in a drive toward that future in which God's kingdom has come nearer? Would the new world, America in particular, recognize that the course of world revolution was involving the western hemisphere already and would continue to do so?

Would the representatives of the 160 member churches now assembling in Evanston be appreciative enough to appraise rightly the great operation undertaken for the sake of the peoples in Asia and Africa who were in ferment? Would Europeans and Americans join to share the spirit of solidarity with those Asians and Africans whose rapid social change had largely come about through the means of western technology, western education, and western religion?

At the opening service in Evanston's First Methodist Church, Dibelius noticed the much-increased number of delegations from Asian countries. The young church was coming into her own. Young leaders of united churches like D. T. Niles of Ceylon and Lesslie Newbigin of South India, surely had a calling to give the marching orders for the second five or six years' period of joint ecumenical action. He was much aware of the growing importance attached to the World Council's East Asia Secretariat in Bangkok, the prospering issue of the Council's official association with the International Missionary Council. There was the prominence of Rajah Manikam, the coming Bishop of India's Lutheran Church, and there was the gracious and most convincing presence of Juhanon Mar Thoma with his apostolic succession of Christ's own apostle to the Indians, deep in legend and in history. They were the focus of attention and world response, and Dibelius admired their prospect in the widening world fellowship. Yet there remained the question where Europe would have her place.

Would Evanston bring to an end the period in which the World Council's Interchurch Aid had supported the peoples of Central Europe and Southeast Asia alike? Ten millon refugees of Europe, ten million refugees of Southeast Asia had been saved from hunger and death at the same time. Had the peoples of Asia, perhaps even the non-Christians among them, manifested a deeper gratitude to the Universal Church? Or was it just the otherness of the young church which, in her local setting, seemed so impressive to the Americans?

Somehow the dormitory assigned to Bishop Dibelius, its very remoteness and dignified distance from Evanston's life centers (McGaw and Sargent Halls on the campus of Northwestern University) seemed symptomatic of a changing scene. Some intimated that by now enough had been done for old and gouty Europe! Had Europe's churchmen to start all over again to tell the painful stories of Soviet Asia's expansion? Had the past which was Europe and the West run its full sweep of hours?

The young leaders entrusted with planning Evanston's double program, including the very instructive one for accredited visitors, gave the delegates who came from Soviet-controlled countries ample scope to tell their new story praising their agreements and concordats with Communist rulers as fully in keeping with God's design for mankind's progress on earth. Again Dibelius meditated how free and independent the witness coming from satellite areas was. Even granted that it would become as independent as the Christian voice still was in Central Germany, would the witness of Germany's eastern neighbors be so genuine as to make the young church of Asia believe that in the very heart of ancient Europe the prophets of communist world revolution were unwillingly providing a strange corrective to the old church's glaring weakness?

The United States Department of State had not made the entry of ecclesiastics from Soviet-controlled countries an easy matter. The Protestants of Poland became the temporary victims of mutual visa restrictions. But their Czech, Slovak, and Hungarian brethren spoke all the louder on what the Soviets had done for the churches by relieving them of the burden of confessional standards and from their traditional leaders. One of the Hungarian delegates who had been raised to episcopal honors after "patiently rendering a helping hand" in the ninety per cent Communist anti-Rajk coup, was so eloquent in uttering eulogies on the unconventional deeds of the new socialist religion that the attention of many uninformed delegates, visitors, and accredited press correspondents grew into curiosity and even into doubt.

The little dormitory in Evanston's Willard Hall which was, in the beginning, a place of gloomy and almost sinister silence, became the scene of prolonged interviews. Not only did American newsmen come to the attic room with their beaming flashlights. Whole units of old world delegations and consultant groups searched after Bishop Dibelius and his assistant, Dr. Günter Jacob of Cottbus, in order to hear what these Germans knew of the progress of religious liberty behind the European iron curtain. Dibelius and Jacob were most reluctant to give answers that might evoke hatred or even antagonism. Equally careful was Eastern Saxony's bishop, the delegate from Dresden. What they all had in mind was but the saying of Paul in a very similar situation: "We can do nothing against the truth" (2 Corinthians 13:8).

CHAPTER EIGHTEEN

Prelude to Balloting

WHEN THE Soviet-supported churchmen from Budapest, Bratislava, and Prague declared in unison that in their countries the Sunday services were overcrowded, the East Germans could only refer to some historic items: More than seventy-five per cent of the churches and chapels formerly belonging to the Protestant churches of East Germany had either been secularized for civic use or handed over to the Roman hierarchy. It was true that inside the Soviet Union proper, the Roman side of the picture was not so terrible. But the overflow of the sanctuaries still open for worship had everywhere a twofold significance. As to the Hungarian rejoicing in the fact that traditional Sunday services were nowhere prohibited, German delegates pointed out that it was indeed no matter of forthright prohibition but of subtle detention. In most factories and agricultural combines, Sunday was a day of registered and better-paid labor. The Young Pioneers, monopoly bearers of youth activities, chose the whole of Sunday morning as the routine period for premilitary exercises, marches, brass-banding, and excursions. When the Soviet-sponsored delegates maintained that no one behind the curtain was arrested for the sake of his convictions or confessions of faith, when they went on to declare that some cases of isolation and imprisonment were due only to individual clergymen's interference with public relations, the East Germans were in a position to reveal how far the functionaries of the totalitarian state and party had lost the capacity to think and to act other than politically. Karl Marx's proposition that all true religion was a private matter for the individual had taken root among the peoples of Russia who had never come to know a preaching or a socially-acting church. As they moved, however, toward the center of Europe, they found the Protestant churches preaching on social and very practical issues, teaching their young generation, and forming fellowships on a non-political and yet very real basis. This was so much against the uniform pattern of the classless society, that the intellectual protagonists of world revolution took any form of religious instruction, Sunday schools and junior Bible classes, as a disguise of deviation and wilful subversion. From the cases of arrested catechists and pastors engaged with home Bible work, Dibelius could prove that throughout his eastern province, the elementary school was already a totalitarian instrument of mind-shaping as rigid as any parochial and sectarian institute could be. One of Eastern Saxony's representatives gave this explanation:

It is very much as it was in the nazi state. One set of ideas becomes orthodoxy with all the authority and pressure of the state machinery behind it. This one-sided teaching is apt to assume the disinterested character of the natural sciences in so far as it makes itself appear "neutral," that is, without presuppositions. The developing of any deviating ideology, especially the maintaining of faith categories not wholly comprehensible by scientific inquiry, is treated as a serious crime. In the more advanced classes, the religion of world communism is still carefully couched in the language of science. Its mission is first spread by an elaborate preaching on the coming golden age of collective society and, at the final stage of high school education, the essence of the quasi-religion is revealed by subversive devices and political adventures calculated to make trouble for the great countries which still stand in the way of world revolution.

It was only one day before the closing of the Evanston Assembly when Dibelius himself took the platform. He did not think it was his calling to sharpen the issues to such a degree that the already subdued Christians of Russia and China would be forever discouraged to seek a spiritual home in that fellowship which was called the World Council of Churches. He knew that Russia's and China's churchmen were not free to express their gratitude to the World Council. He welcomed all the more the Council's appeal to non-member churches drawn up by that unfailing supporter of minorities, Bishop Bell of Chichester, in the Assembly section dealing with international relations. Dibelius' feelings for the faithful and persevering peasant people of Greater Russia had strongly grown with his expectation that the hour was not so distant when the eastern hemisphere would be governed by men putting the welfare of their unpretending people above world conquest.

So what East Germany's main speaker did in the first thirteen days of the great Evanston Assembly was nothing more than to answer quietly and factually the questions evoked by overstatements from some of the more conspicuous delegates. As we have seen, the more sonorous were largely two groups of delegates: (1) Czechoslovak and Hungarian Christians who had evidently lost the capacity to judge persons and events in a global and truly ecumenical perspective; and (2) native Christians from the Southeast Asian subcontinent. The second group was rather tempted and, by some advanced Protestants of America, even encouraged to dramatize some of the disputed records of French, Dutch, and British colonialism. They thought they would do well to accept the Soviet liberators' well-formulated promises at their face value. At the end of the Assembly, some of those anti-Western enthusiasts came to see more clearly and admitted they had become more or less unwillingly the unpaid partners in a world-wide conspiracy of silence and untruth about the real situation of the Christian community within the totalitarian orbit.

In this regard and in others too, Evanston proved to be much more than a series of confessional contests, more also than an array of spectacles with the President of the United States and the General Secretary of the United Nations acting as paramount performers. To the Christians of East and Central Germany, Evanston emerged as the reassuring test of what William Temple had envisaged as the one great fact of the twentieth century: churches, denominations, missionary societies, indigenous communities of less developed continents, and even such long-separated units as the Salvation Army and the Society of Friends were growing together in an organic process without any hurtful disregard of their innate growing-potential.

The whole witness of growth and togetherness had something outgoing and unprecedented in it. Kenneth T. Henderson, the pioneer of Australian laymen, rightly pointed out that "there was much more blood in Evanston" than there was at previous gatherings of the World Council.[1] As Dibelius came to set his eyes on both Australia and Southeast Asia, he found he could not evaluate Evanston by any better words than his fellow-pilgrim from the southern hemisphere was to formulate:

The quest of fellowship and truth will not stop short of the reuniting of Christendom in a church that gives life to the special virtues and insights developed in the divided communities, a church with prophetic and sacramental ministries acceptable to all, a church with complete freedom of "walk about" for individuals. As our satisfaction in self-sufficiency dissolves and humility becomes the driving force of the ecumenical movement, so will the possibility of such a church loom. That state of things is foreshadowed in what we have today. It will be part of the discipline to worship part of the time in the areas of the church that are comparatively strange to us and to listen to voices uttering thoughts we find difficult to understand. Meantime we must not feel frustrated because we in our own hearts are so distant from such a vision. Let us proceed in fellowship in Christ, through difference aiming at a resolution of difference by surrender to his Spirit. And let us eschew theories which give final sanction to our divided communities as they are.

---

[1] *Christian Century*, March 14, 1956.

Though he spent most of his Evanston time in informal talks, Dibelius made it clear to his American friends that the *status quo*, the divided state of Christendom, was the greatest possible hindrance to the dynamic intent of God's Spirit moving in the history of mankind. Seldom if ever before were the divergent camps of rigid confessionalists and free-lance enthusiasts brought together to a common evaluation of statism and the state as they were on the eve before the final day of the Evanston Assembly. The event that brought unanimous reaction came as a surprise to Dibelius himself. He was not supposed to have anything to do with the structure and future functioning of the World Council. Nor had he been invited to be on any committee nominating the officers for the Council's second period. But he was requested to address the plenary meeting finally on "The Church's Dependence on God and Her Independence from Man." After all the questions posed as a repercussion of Far Eastern and satellite statements, Dibelius found sufficient time to rethink and reformulate what he had to proclaim. He started by recalling the strange fact that, in the twentieth century, his country was the first to witness an open persecution of the Christian Church and to produce martyrs destined to die for their confession of faith. He repeated the grave words of protest uttered by the Synod of Barmen against Hitler's and Himmler's aggressive pseudo-religion:

We reject the false doctrine that the church, as a source of her proclamation should recognize outside or alongside the word of God still other events and powers, forces and truths, as God's revelation. We reject the false doctrine that the state, above and beyond its special task, should become the only and total order of human life.

Having explained how this Declaration of Barmen attained ecumenical stature in twenty years' time, Dibelius went on to say:

We in Germany still stand in full unanimity behind these words of the Resistance Synod, whether we be Lutherans or Reformed or belong to the United Church, whether we happen to live in East or West Germany. The church has to obey God rather than men, in the name of Jesus Christ. For this conviction we went to prison and to the concentration camps.

In our secular time, state and politics are the most powerful factors in the life of each nation. Whether the church remains steadfast here, whether it remains independent from the state, its propaganda and its political will, there its destiny will be decided. The basic test for the church's freedom will come in the moment when the state declares itself a totalitarian state. And be it noted that there is a totalitarian climate not only in Europe, but also in other parts of the globe!

Let us not think that a totalitarian state will permit the churches to organize the freedom of its members to sacrifice in such a way as is common in the Anglo-Saxon countries. The temporal power expects its citizens to sacrifice exclusively for state purposes and not for the church. She is not permitted to enter the homes to collect the contributions of the faithful. Therefore the church must discover new ways to carry her life through times of testing.

He who works with the church in totalitarian surroundings will always have the most limited material assets. If you enter state service, if you work in the spirit of state propaganda, then you will receive four times the amount of your former income and will be able to support your children without worry.

There is much quiet martyrdom in all churches which live under a totalitarian regime. Those people, however, who have the strength for this quiet martyrdom, are the ones who preserve the church's independence.

Independence from man and dependence on God alone can grow into the church only from within. She must daily plunge into the word of God; she has to be at home in the world of the sacraments. Daily she must pray to God to be at her side with his Holy Spirit. This praying is of basic and decisive significance, especially for this reason: the temptation of Jesus Christ is continued in the history of his church. Only after the church becomes independent from the worry over daily bread, independent from the danger of conceit, independent from every aspiration toward external power, only then can she rest assured that the Spirit of Christ is with her still. Only then may she refer to herself, in humble confidence, the sacred words: "The devil leaves, and behold, angels came and ministered" (Matthew 4:11).

Meanwhile there comes from within the world where earthly dependence constantly increases a great yearning, that there shall be one place in this world where liberty becomes apparent, the kingly liberty of those who find themselves bound only to their heavenly Lord. If the church lives up to that call and yearning, then she is at any rate—no matter what her tradition and structure may have been in other respects—a living witness to the fact that there is the reality of another world, a world over which the state possesses no power, a world which sets a limitation to the state's totalitarian demands.

The state is really totalitarian only when the church, as a church, no longer exists within its orbit. If God grants his grace, this shall nowhere happen. It will never happen where the Church Universal is alive.

No one who has not lived in a totalitarian state has any conception how heavily the timely burden rests upon the faithful. Their constant prayer is that God may keep them free from fear of men when making their decisions, so that it becomes apparent also to the opponent. The church does not act from political reflection, but under the word of God. Her ardent desire is that even the enemy may be brought under the power of his word and spirit.

There is one great thing, however, others may and can do: they can permit us to ask from them the one thing for which Paul the Apostle asked the congregation of enslaved Christians in imperial Rome: "That ye strive together with me in your prayers to God and for me" (Romans 15:30).

The thundering applause which, after unprecedented moments of deep silence, filled the spacious interior of Evanston's McGaw Hall expressed the unalloyed satisfaction of many thousands and the natural surprise of some hundreds besides.

That last Sunday of the World Assembly was indeed a day

which God's gathered people would "rejoice and be glad in, because the Lord made it." The old world's burden had not been carried in vain. Nova Scotia's Nicholson and Alberta's Robison were the first delegates to express the listeners' deep satisfaction over the serene approach which prevailed in the speaker's factual survey of the frontier situation.

The World Assembly's hopes were indeed not left unfulfilled. The tensions of evil were now forced to be on the defensive, and the prospect which Norway's Eivind Berggrav had envisaged when he introduced Otto Dibelius from the chair became reality. Bishop Berggrav said he trusted the church family of Christians would go on changing the atmosphere of the whole world. The family had gathered in the morning of that day for a service of Holy Communion conducted according to the rites of the Church of South India. Berggrav and Dibelius had been sitting next to each other when the celebrants, C. K. Jacob and Lesslie Newbigin, called on the large congregation to recall Christ's great desire to manifest brotherly reconciliation before offering alms in his presence. It was indeed a revival of the early Christians' holy kiss of agape when Peace was given from one worshiper to another, the giver devoutly placing his right hand against the right palm of the receiver and each closing his left over the other's right hand. The celebrants also reminded the gathering that the sacrifice to be offered after Peace had been given with the greeting of charity and love was oneness in Christ. In St. Augustine's adaptation of scriptural words, the sacrifice offered in peace and reconciliation was the oneness of them that were sometimes in darkness but were now light in the Lord, reproving the works of disruption and walking together as children of light.

What a reassuring act of intercommunion: the Indian Bishop Jacob, as main celebrant assisted by Bishop Newbigin, once a missionary come from a nation which had long ruled India by rigid colonial methods. What a hopeful sign to see Berggrav, the long-imprisoned victim of the German Nazis, now exchanging holy agape with Dibelius who had strangely suffered from Nazis of his own surroundings.

Right indeed was the Anglican observer who saw in the fine and happy Sunday afternoon the fruitful issue of a radiant morning. It was also right to observe that the prolonged applause for Berlin's presiding bishop was given "in token of standing beside him spiritually in his struggle." The account which Dibelius gave of the continued struggle, on Evanston's third and last Sunday, appealed to all present as a genuine concern for the visible united church.

Not that he permitted himself to wander in the vacuous heights of an empty enthusiasm. He made it abundantly clear that peace in the presence of Christ is not necessarily identical with the unyielding atmosphere of a Trappist convent or the suppressed whispering of a prison. Nor was reconciliation set forth as an easy excuse for glossing over the fundamentals in human thought and action. History envisaged with Christ is, in the end, more salutary than the various movements which men carry out in their gruesome lust for self-glorification. But just as Christ became man, entering even the most dismal areas of human affairs, so also the subsequent history of the people called Christians is animated by much drama and dialectic.

In the movement for church unity the period of Evanston was in many respects a creative pause, a time given to the pledge of rethinking, recasting, and relearning the promising course of history's drama. Quite a few of the drama's conscious partners sensed the utter newness of the day. The ghastly night show manager, "that weird and horrible phenomenon of human life called the totalitarian state," was being toppled from his eminence. How it was done was unprecedented and, therefore, unexpected by historians and theologians alike.

Before the last Sunday came to an end, there were still some delegates who had their own reflections on the firm and well-studied manner in which East Germany's traditional leader had been moved forward by invisible hands to remove the masks of counter-acting persons and configurating forces. Thinking in terms of earthly development, they were apt to stress the interacting roles of geography and continental history. For the unavoidable task of recasting the cultural and spiritual forces of

Europe, they might have preferred any delegate to the one who had more than once represented Old Protestant East Germany. Like prisoners of unredeemed actions, they would not even trust a reborn church in the heart of Europe. Instead of rising to a redemptive partnership in the making of a new history directed at the New Creation, they wondered why it should be that old history was out of focus, too disabled now to take its chartered revenge. Agitated Europeans of the continent's western parts were sitting together with Christians of all continents, having on a platform in front of them a leader whom jaunty contemporaries had described as being an unswerving conservative, a man of "tradition only." But was it sheer traditionalism that they heard proclaimed, this freedom of the church, her independence from the self-assertive earthly factors in human history?

No, the time had come in which the old labels *conservative* and *mere traditionalist* did not fit any longer. The Dibelius of Evanston in 1954 was the same Dibelius who had signed Germany's first Declaration of National Repentance twelve years before.

When preparations were being made for the Evanston assembly Edmund Schlink of Heidelberg, one of the more scholarly supporters of Otto Dibelius, had ably anticipated the German churches' solidarity with the younger churches who "are determined to forget those things which are behind and to reach forth to those things which are before."[2]

We are assembled here as divided churches. But the Lord who will come again stands before us all, whether we realize it or not. We are already in the net which he has cast out, even if this net has not yet been drawn out of the sea and we may still imagine we are swimming about freely and gaily in the water. However much we may be divided among ourselves, we are in fact one, because we are surrounded inescapably by the one net and

---

[2] Phil. 3:13, quoted by Edmund Schlink at the Third World Conference on Faith and Order preparing for the Second Assembly of the World Council of Churches, reprinted in *Ecumenical Review*, vol. 5, pp. 27 ff.

because we shall be delivered up to the one Lord and Fisherman.

It may happen then that great and proud churches, which seemed to be firmly built, collapse like a pack of cards, and only a small remnant of them perseveres in face of temptation. Parishes which have a reputation for being alive suddenly prove to be dead.[3] Leading churchmen to whom Christians used to look for guidance suddenly have no more words of relief, comfort, and advice for their flock. Changes of an unforeseen kind then take place. The first are the last and the last first.

At the same time, however, the dividing walls between churches of different confessions become strangely transparent. That which is great comes forth from the small, the One from the many.

In Evanston, the members of the first presidium of the World Council resigned, in accordance with the provisions of the constitution adopted in Amsterdam. Now a Scandinavian delegate strongly suggested that of the two archbishops who had served as presidents, at least the Anglican should be authorized to stand for re-election. A dramatic turn evolved from the suggestion. Anglicans, Old Catholics, and some Lutherans were keen on advocating the blessings of episcopal leadership in historic succession. A smaller number of Lutherans and all of what the Europeans called Free Churches went along with the Methodists, whose tenacious leader, Bishop G. Bromley Oxnam, contended that the constitutional issue must be related to the fundamental claim that the coming great church should be envisaged as a prophetic and dynamic body, open to constant renewal in leadership and members. The Methodists pleaded it would be incompatible with the sacred concept of the forward-moving pilgrim church if the assembly elected a presidium as another time-serving instrument of ecclesiastical statesmanship.

No, the assembly was still not ready to vote. The third Sunday was over, but the debate went on. A further delaying move was to come from a more neutralist camp. It was one of the Swiss

---

[3] Revelation 3:1.

delegates who thought the hour had come to urge that, if any person from the European continent was to have a place in the new presidium, it would be useful to elect a layman.

A Swiss motion to reconsider Otto Dibelius' nomination to an office in the presidium was carried by a vote of 158 to 146, with several abstentions. The members of the nominating committee conferred most conscientiously with the delegates who had witnessed the debate and the vote without taking the floor. American members of the important committee made it their special concern to hear the opinions of delegates from Central European areas. Not only from Berliners and East Germans, but also from Austrians and Scandinavians they gained the impression that it was something infinitely greater than a strategy of prestige or power to regard German's senior delegate as a new incorporation of Europe's inheritance and Europe's hope.

Here then was a man who had the experience and inspiration of wholehearted resistance to three authoritarian movements whose protagonists had claimed or were still claiming absolute and total loyalty from the peoples of Europe. He had faced the strange revival of a crusade to rebuild a kind of Holy Roman Empire. He had faced and greatly challenged the Nordic race religion with all its Fascist and Nazi devices. He was now encountering the most gigantic progeny that the philosophers of his own nation had brought into being. His imposing counterparts in the ultimate strife for the life and soul of Europe were the heralds of the world revolution, still very much in the ascendant.

Though there was some apparent logic in the move to have lay representation in the World Council's presidium, the Assembly became increasingly impressed with the sense of urgency and transcendent hope expressed in the witness of Europe's frontier people to their present leader. When it came to the final decision, it was no longer a mere matter of form. Too many voters realized that at this election much of Europe's inner freedom and inner continuity was at stake. With a noble restraint, the nominating committee declared how long and carefully they had reconsidered their first choice and why they could not take the responsibility for any other selection. So Dibelius' name was presented again. Moments of tension followed. Then the vote was taken. Not only Germans and Austrians, but all Hungarians, all Czechs and Slovaks, all French and Dutch, all British and Scandinavian delegates present raised their hands to join in the American proposal to elect the whole presidium as proposed by the nominating committee. Once more the names were read: Scotland's John Baillie, the Methodist world church's Uberto Barbieri, Germany's Otto Dibelius, India's Juhanon Mar Thoma, the Orthodox Sobornost's Archbishop Michael, and Henry Knox Sherrill, Presiding Bishop of America's Protestant Episcopal Church. The vote was unanimous.

While he was still in Evanston Dibelius received words of congratulation from the two German camps which lived divided against each other through the tension of cold war. The Chancellor of Federal Germany worded his acknowledgment in much the same way as the Vice-Premier of East Germany's Democratic Republic. One of the left-wing German weekly news magazines, usually not in great favor with the church, made this statement:

Dibelius owes his world renown to his continued ministry to east and west. In his independent stewardship there is a most beneficial interacting of history at large and a personality convincing even in the most individual little features of life. He is undeviating and yet suggestive and very human.

More patriotic newspapers thought the hour had come for them to rejoice in Germany's return to the scene of world events. Dibelius made it clear that he would have nothing to do with the exuberant flow of words prepared by western press correspondents. He thought of his new ecumenical office more in terms of a European obligation than as a personal tribute. And surely this was not a time to rest on laurels.

CHAPTER NINETEEN

Raking Up the Embers

WHILE DIBELIUS was still in Evanston, the whole of America was taken by surprise when the news came that France had voted down the European Defense Community. Perhaps he knew better than many Americans how elaborately the professionals of world revolution were working at the heart of France, feeding on the successive and ever-weakening governments in Paris. It appeared that the vacillations and labors of France resulted from cultural and spiritual discontinuity. For over a hundred years some of the best elements, the faithful Protestants, had been driven to Germany, Holland, and America. The anarchic principles of 1789 did futile violence to the nation's past, and no genuine part of the Christian Church had ever become reconciled with the fanatic Jacobins' heritage, rationalism, and state socialism. Whenever he saw signs of a Christian renewal in France, Dibelius did what he could to strengthen them. He had recently praised the noble work of the French priest-workers in his sermon on the first Sunday in Lent, preached in East Berlin.[1] But he knew they were a small minority, and he was not surprised when he heard of the increasing

---

[1] Sermon on Matthew 4:4 in St. Mary's, East Berlin, March 7, 1954.

hardships they had to experience from their own superiors.

Faithful Christians in the Federal German government wondered if the European Defense Community had not collapsed for the very reason that it was in the French manner, so much preoccupied with security measures. If the Macedonian call had been uttered for all Europeans, there was work to be done. Europeans had seen their ancient pagan empires falling to pieces; they had witnessed the violent disasters of many revolutions. Yet the Church of Christ had survived. Reborn under the pains of two world wars, Christians of different lands and creeds were growing together. A wide ministry of laymen offered its help in the task of wholesome reconstruction. Surely this was a time to build up in Europe "a spiritual house" which would extend across the ancient barriers of realms and nations.

The spiritual house once envisaged by St. Peter was to Dibelius not a mirage of the future. To him it was rather a model for the new order of the ages which the people of God were chosen to set forth, declaring the wonderful deeds of him who calls the pilgrims and indeed all men of patience out of darkness into his marvelous light.

When he came back from Evanston to Berlin, he heard that the stream of refugees leaving the Eastern zone of Germany had greatly increased. The refugee camps of Berlin's American sector were filled not only by individuals persecuted for their religious convictions, but also by opportunists who did not want to earn their daily bread by honest work. To counteract this movement of irresponsible East-West migration, Dibelius made his letter acknowledging the East German government's congratulation on the Evanston election a starting point for new and fruitful negotiations. Being now the representative of all the continent's non-Roman churches in the World Council's presidium, he gave to the left-wing government of East Berlin a great chance to prove their readiness for readjusting the East to the reborn spirit of a Christian Europe. He solemnly proclaimed that the western churches would henceforth encourage no citizen of Soviet-controlled countries to leave his work or residence.

He was naturally willing to apply the great means of welfare and brotherly relief to exiles who could prove that they were in real danger. But even among those exiles he promised to have the solid and morally reliable ones approached to see whether they would consider resuming their eastern work after a certain time. With the help of the Commission on World Service of the National Council of the Churches of Christ in the United States, he organized a recreation center and retreat for the continued counseling and strengthening of those who might be ready to renew their essential witness to a Christian order of life within the orbit of communism, the "world sphere of the gigantic failure."

All this widening of foundations and premises was not merely a gesture, much less a piece of propaganda for curious onlookers. No, he made it a special point to pay his first personal foreign visit, as a newly elected President of the World Council, to the churches of Czechoslovakia. Nazi rule in that country had been an imposition of pagan customs for seven years of unprecedented horrors. But the Protestants, Catholics, and Jews of Czechoslovakia realized that the torturers who had delt with their nation were the same who had been mishandling Otto Dibelius and Reinold von Thadden, who went with him to Prague in the first winter after Evanston. The snowy streets of the Czech capital were lined with expectant and appreciative crowds. The students of the Protestant Comenius Faculty gave to Dibelius and von Thadden a joyous welcome. The president of the State Commission for Religious Affairs, Dr. Havelka, gave them a very civil reception. The Bishop of Leitmeric was moved to tears when Dibelius inquired after the whereabouts of Joseph Beran, the completely isolated Archbishop of Prague. Another Roman Catholic, Dr. Mara of the National Welfare Conference, said no one had dared to make such an inquiry or to mention Joseph Beran's name for years. The Reformed Bishop Varga was careful in his ways of expression, but the sincerity and warmth of his heart were as reassuring as they had been in Evanston a few months before.

Czechoslovakia's Protestant minority churches appeared to

be not without financial support from public revenues. But the support implied elaborate restriction with respect to every program of extension. Of the graduates and undergraduates who wished to take up training for holy orders, only fifteen per cent were admitted to the state-controlled seminaries, and there were no other institutions for the purpose.

Yet the students were hopeful and cheered Berlin's bishop very warmly. In Prague's Church of the Vineyard, he had preached to them on Peter's saying, "We are ransomed from the futile" (1 Peter 1:18, 19). The students echoed the sermon's closing words when they accompanied Dibelius back to Ruziné Airport:

We are redeemed indeed, but it should appear more clearly in us that we are redeemed. The world shall come to perceive it.

The one thing Dibelius could not find out from the Czechs, nor even from the southern Slovak churchmen of Hungarian descent, was the actual condition of the minority groups inside the new boundaries of the Hungarian People's Republic. Hungary's delegation to Evanston had been less homogeneous than that of Czechoslovakia. He welcomed all the more the resolution of the subsequent meeting of the World Council to convene the Council's Central Committee in the summer of 1956 at Galyatetö, a resort some 2000 feet above the city of Budapest.

The decision to go right into Hungary and to invite to the Budapest meeting Chinese and Russian Christians of various denominations was taken in Davos, Switzerland, where the leaders of the World Council met at the same time when President Eisenhower and Marshall Bulganin were holding their Summit Conference in nearby Geneva. The churches were going to devote more than one year to work out the fundamental priorities in a common desire to lay the basis of understanding.

Since there were Christians not only in Czechoslovakia and Hungary, but also in the more distant parts of the eastern hemisphere, it seemed only proper to acknowledge that members of the world church were living in a give-and-take situation. Without being interested in any red carpet rolled out for him behind the curtain, Dibelius took a lively interest in his discovery that God was very much present and potent in Soviet life.

The meeting in Davos near Geneva was the Central Committee's first gathering that he attended as one of the World Council's presidents. There he did not speak mainly as a German. Until the great last day of the meeting, he listened much more than he talked. He found it most helpful to listen to the Asian partners of the church, to Charles Malik of Lebanon, D. T. Niles of Ceylon, and Lesslie Newbigin of the rising Church of South India. In view of Russia's and almost all Asia's outcry that Europe's and America's churches were merely fighting the battle of western imperialism, the insight of men like Malik and Niles was very reassuring. They were warmhearted and very convincing advocates of the churches' indigenization, while the official schools of western diplomacy still continued to quote the rational argument of Arnold Toynbee, whose philosophy was that Asia had "but one choice, to accept all or nothing of western civilization."

The political leaders of Asia and Africa had met a few months before at Bandung in Indonesia. They had proclaimed the "independent progress of the two continents." But was there reality and hope in Asia's and Africa's independence? The leading delegate from the Dominion of Ceylon had expressed rather a deviating prospect.

The pointedly tolerant spirit of the Summit Conference at Geneva was culminating in the device of two world systems coexisting peacefully at any cost. But was there reality and hope for the peoples of three big continents affected by the Geneva resolutions? Some of the American delegates to the conference honestly admitted that many burning questions of East and West alike remained wholly unsettled. But the very questions asked in the presence of leading Chinese and Russians revealed the challenge evolving from the change of the world scene.

The political conference in Geneva and the church leaders' meeting in Davos ended almost at the same time. The World Council's Central Committee asked Bishop Dibelius to give the final address. These were his words:

Nothing is more characteristic of the present age than the fact that the peoples of the earth have begun to concern themselves with mankind's final issues. They ask mankind's age-old question, "What are we here for anyway?"

We have passed the stage when each nation could think of itself as the focal point of the whole world, when nations could consider themselves justified in waging war every ten or twenty years in order to increase their power at the expense of weaker neighbors, each time leaving 20,000 or 20,000,000 men dead on the battlefield. Men are beginning to realize that it is the most vulgar and shoddy of all ambitions to desire power gained by force over others, whether individuals or nations.

But if that is no longer an aim in life, what is there left? Have we come to the point where the nations have no meaning but are simply subdivisions in a great, undifferentiated sprawl of humanity? It might almost seem so. With the buildings of today—waterworks, atomic piles, technical colleges, and so on—one can never tell whether the buildings belong to Russia or to America, to Rio de Janeiro or to Calcutta.

Our ways of speech are becoming ever more technical and standardized. Our modes of dress are becoming uniform. Our very thoughts are becoming standardized. Does it not seem that the time is near when the five continents will be peopled by a single, leveled-off mass of humanity? Such is the question of the nations today. They ask the Church of Christ.

The church can answer only with the gospel. For the gospel is the only thing that she has. And the gospel says that God placed the nations in the world "that they might feel for him and grasp him and in that way find him."

In keeping with the gospel the church goes on to answer: Build your atomic piles and your spaceships. Turn the deserts of the earth into blossoming gardens. Conduct microbiological research into the origins of diseases—each nation in its own way, according to its talents and resources. But remember that it is God who permits you gradually to enter into the innermost secrets of his creation. Sing then his praises in humility and gratitude.

Make your welfare state. But do not forget that there is a distinction between a hospital being a repair-shop for the upkeep of a country's labor force or a place where care is given to both body and soul as components of a divine image.

Do not forget that it makes a difference whether the upbringing of the young develops in them a readiness to help those who are in need or whether all this is left to public welfare departments which have signboards over their office doors with words like these: Please deposit your soul in the cloakroom!

In an epigraph to one of his Russian folk-tales, Count Tolstoy says, "Where love is, there also is God." Where love counts for anything, there we may feel and find the Lord. There the question as to the meaning of life is answered, and all nations can join in praising him who is love in action.

In making that answer of the church acceptable, you will not succeed alone. None of us will. We know what is wrong with each of us. That is why we have come together, that our churches may learn from one another how to make our faith richer, our love more burning, our obedience to God's laws more perfect— so that we may be able to present to the nations this source of inspiration better than before, more acceptably than before.

May I recall here the inspiring words which Charles Malik of Lebanon spoke to us in Evanston—words of which we were justly reminded in a moving hour only recently:

"What the eastern world needs, is something other than what it has been offered so far, something infinitely more humble, more positively outreaching, something capturing the hearts of men, touching their need for fellowship and understanding, their deep desire for being included and being trusted—something providing them with real hope, hope for themselves and their children, hope in this life as well as in the next. Something of this order is needed. This Something is Jesus Christ, the risen Lord." The peoples ask and the church answers with Christ.

None of the ninety members of the World Council's Central Committee could get away from the strangely soft and relaxing atmosphere of Switzerland without the striking assurance that the man who had been given a new office in Evanston was changing and growing in stature.

Growth in historic insight is always indicative of new inroads for the eternal factors of life on this earth. A reality greater and deeper than superficial onlookers can evaluate gets hold of a man conscious of being a person. A real person is never self-sufficient, but always an instrument of some divine intent. A person in that sense prefers an inward experience to the allegedly safer viewing of historic events from the outside.

As a person reborn, widened in his horizon and given a new scope and field of action, Dibelius was more and more fascinated by Russia's and all Asia's challenging transformation. He urgently felt that the widening of his concern was bound to make him rethink all Christian strategy in light of the global change implied in the eastern challenge.

If the World Council were in a position to receive eastern Orthodox Christians as equal members willing and able to contribute to the world church their awareness of eternity, their deeply human sense of mystery, what an enriching experience it would be on both sides! Surely that was a church of sacrificial love and sacramental beauty which had managed to survive three decades of systematic disabling, disowning, and disconcerting. How friendly and outgoing were the looks in the eyes of the Orthodox priests with whom Dibelius held regular services of ecumenical worship in Hope Church and St. Mary's, both in East Berlin! If the century of the church was to incorporate the era of coexistence of East and West, surely the revered tradition of Russia's Holy Synod and the spirituality of contemplative life would find their proper place and reassessment.

With Charles Malik, the Orthodox churchman of Lebanon, Dibelius fully agreed that the roots of our century's anti-Christian concepts were not to be sought in the hearts of the Russian people, but rather in the past of Western Germany where Catholic culture had provided but a loose framework for the life of the people. He also agreed with the contents of Malik's second Evanston lecture quoted at Davos and had the following quotations translated into several continental languages:

Ours is a novel situation; it is utterly unprecedented. Because it involves radical adjustments on a world-wide scale—adjustments in military and strategic concepts, in political alignments; because this technological revolution is not at an end but becomes in effect more and more revolutionary every day, every day upsetting the balance that was struck before, every day liquifying some crucial situation that was supposed to have been more or less frozen and stabilized only the night before: because there is the danger of the revolution getting out of control, of its doing so in the face of more or less relative darkness as to the real state of the possible enemy—it may be another two or three years before responsible leadership gets the situation in hand.

Surely one must not rake up the embers of the past. But there are two kinds of past—a past that is entirely dead and had better be forgotten, and a past that is very living indeed. The living past is such that you do not need at all to rake up its embers, for it is itself raking you up all the time, and if you do not bestir yourself while it is at you, you are dead. Karl Marx and Marxism-Leninism do not belong to the dead past whose embers should not be disturbed.

Above and beyond any difficulty in the political and disarmament field, and ultimately conditioning every such difficulty, is the great estrangement in the realm of the mind and the spirit. Dialectical materialism teaches precisely that contradiction and conflict are of the essence. Therefore, what is needed is a theoretical and spiritual overcoming of Karl Marx.

When the Marxist scientists and theoreticians accept the challenge of conferring at length with responsible thinkers of the non-communist world; when their textbooks have been altered with respect to the ultimacy of the class struggle, the necessity of war and world revolution; when honor is given to the existence of absolute truth, the power of the mind to grasp it, the glory and necessity of freedom, and the character of whatever ultimate reality there is; when we are sure that profound modifications of doctrine are taking place with respect to these ultimate themes, then the world may look forward to the possibility of a new dawn.

CHAPTER TWENTY

More Is Committed

FOR EUROPE and the Middle East, the effect of Charles Malik's translated statement was astounding in many ways. Some enthusiasts and well-meaning pacifists thought him too stubbornly intent on tracing God's guidance in the history of the non-communist nations. Malik, they said, had paid too little attention to "the wondrous accomplishments of modern Israelis" which they, the enthusiasts, believed to be in the direct lineal descent of God's holy covenant people.

The more traditional theologians found Malik too boldly related to the *last things*, to utopian dreams and eschatological hopes. But in the center of the acidulous dispute about the World Council's "slow and sloping ascent from Evanston's Northwestern low and humid pastures to the Davosion snow on the summit," there stood out one solid point of practicable departure: a purified church's sober concern for the reality of the spiritual realm.

In a talk to some American interviewers at Davos, Dibelius was forthright enough to state that from a Summit Conference he did not so much expect a static peace, but outgoing concerns for any people of goodwill, concerns for a new future rather than fixed perpetuations of established precedents:

Being on a summit, I like to feel the breeze of altitude and independence. There is a good saying by one of the young Indian bishops: Some strong blasting is vital for any scene-shifting. History cannot near its acceptable hour, unless we Christian fellow-laborers do the shifting and the moving. So why not set the stage of human history in joyful obedience to the dictates of truth revealed in the Son of man?

Independence always implies a move and a venture, a whole-hearted thrust into the future.

Independence remains the saintly privilege of God's fellow-laborers, if only they don't forget that he is the author of peace, not of disorder nor of confusion.[1]

On the true summit, there is man's dependence on God alone. Where the heights of a universal historical responsibility under God are seen and reckoned with, there the Lord of History will make the leaders of the nations find the salutary ways, the ways to human solidarity and uncorrupted stability.

Greatly daring, the German bishop claimed that the ways of Christ in the twentieth century are more deeply concerned with the personal history of man than the devices of modern democracy have so far been. When he returned from Davos to Berlin, he had an inspiring visit from a man equally young and vigorous as Malik, also equally interested in the trends of the rising East and the new ways of Asia. The interesting visitor who called on him was a representative of Church World Service, the American Reginald H. Helfferich. He came to report to the new Joint President on a research tour he had made for the World Council to India, Pakistan, Malaya, Indonesia, Hong Kong, and Korea. His new experience was to find the scattered family of Christian people persecuted for their faith in many parts of Asia.

In Celebes, formerly a great colony in the Netherlands East Indies, Helfferich was able to meet three leaders of a church numbering some 60,000 who had sought and found some safety in the deep jungle of that Indonesian island. There had been

---

[1] 1 Cor. 14:32.

acts of crucifixion, of beheading, and of tearing faithful individuals asunder between gored oxen. There was hunger to the
point of starvation, and it was difficult to carry food or medicines
through the barrier of the pagan terrorists.

Yet the church in Celebes did not sink into despondency.
While they deplored that a great number of white missionaries
had left the island when the Dutch crown no longer offered them
a safe-guard against resurgent paganism, they held fast to the
promise that the gates of hell would not prevail and that the
Christian God was not an author of confusion, but of peace.
They were filled with new joy since the World Council of
Churches had heard of their plight and had sent an ambassador
bearing greetings of love and compassion, at the same time offering needed assistance. While material support was badly needed,
the leaders of this persecuted church assured their visiting
brother that of far greater importance was the enduring of sympathy and the growing solidarity across the sea.

The ecumenical reporter went on to say:

> The thing which encourages the Christians of Southeast Asia
> is the mere fact that they are not forgotten. The very knowledge
> that they are in the love and concern of unknown brothers gives
> them the feeling that all around there is our family of Christ.
> They have come to rejoice in a partnership comprehending
> more than just the elements of the lofty Dutch and the lowly
> forsaken Celebese.

Such an insight indicated a profound change in that missionary relationship which had too often prevailed in the white triumph of the past. As Dibelius heard the returning ally reporting
on the Indonesian encounter, he had a conviction that the
dangerous advance to that dark jungle area was, in fact, a blessed
shaft of light presaging the dawning of the day to come. Surely
the midnight hour in which Reginald Helfferich held that unusual meeting in the shadows of exotic trees, was a silent symbol of a triumphant fact. When the jungle meeting took place,
it was still dark. But the old world order of forsakenness and
inferiority was no more.

Though the jungle is still the jungle, though the barrier is impenetrable for much material aid, love has reached across. To the hearts of their hurt and haunted people, the returning leaders of the forest church have been taking back new tidings of hope. The morrow after those talks in the shadows was different.

Indeed, on every morning now, these people in the woods can greet the day with the awareness of Christ's family encircling the earth with the power of his love.

The new member of the World Council's presidium was keen to observe that the Church of Christ was no longer seen as a decorative annex of the secular powers. So far the policy-making powers of Asia had not paid much attention to the Christian efforts moving away from the outmoded policy of pressure and retaliation. Now, however, it became evident that the pressure from the pagan native forces was as inhuman and un-Christian as the former rule of the secular white "foreigner" could ever have been. The true church had to denote both of them as restraining and deforming factors in history.

It was no longer surprising then that the Celebese Christians should be interested to hear of the intercession, of the multitude of prayers rising in distant areas where brothers were waking up to realize that "God made foolish the wisdom of the world." What seemed to be abnormal in the eyes of the world became normal now, and even "necessary in the eyes of all Christians on the growing edge."

So perverted seemed the minds of the mighty that whole governments were at a loss when the masses of Asia grew restive as nowhere else in the world. Helfferich had seen refugees dying of starvation in a camp at the edge of Karachi when, at the same time, mountains of wheat imported from the United States of America perished as a consequence of bad and irresponsible handling. If here and at other points of utter helplessneess, the churches did not see their essential Christ-given task of the diaconate, the word of God was of no avail. The gospel was not presented in all its fulness when its preaching did not issue in the immediate interacting of Christian men standing in solidarity over against the incompassionate rule of the secular forces old and new.

The field was white unto the harvest, and in many eastern lands the soil was being reddened with martyrs' blood. The church was indeed on the growing edge of Christendom. With the helping counselor and friend who had been to the Far East from the golden West, Berlin's bishop agreed that the fellowship of the concerned was bound to become a family of indigenous churches with members of equal standing, of giving and taking, of sharing and interceding, in East Germany, in India and Pakistan, in Indonesia, and in both the Koreas.

Always prepared for God's new acts in human history, the Bishop realized that Europe's attention to the new ecumenical leadership could be turned into an instrument of healing and sharing. Speaking of interchurch relations across the continents, he still did not think highly of any association of equal partners in disproportionate ratios, as advocated in some of the artificial schemes of reunion:

Creative unity is more than a matter of doctrine. It is primarily a subject of prayer. United in a common purpose of prayer, we become partakers of Christ's compassion with all his Father's travailed creation. From that compassion is flowing our holy desire to do good to all men, and especially to those who are of the household of faith. The household of God will be fully restored if its manifold members are reconciled through a service of united world action flowing from the prayers uttered by ourselves in spiritual communion with Christ and within a fellowship of a common desire and a common concern.

The Christian reconstruction of Europe turned out to be more than a temporary project. From Edinburgh 1910 to Prague 1955, Dibelius' experience of Europe had been one of pain and promise in due succession. The two were interdependent, and the promise was still as potent a force as was the Macedonian call heard anew with all the poignancy of the painfully forsaken and hopefully expectant.

A reborn Europe would include both ancient Macedonia and

Orthodox Greece;[2] it would incorporate the whole Mediterranean in spite of Italy's rising anticlericalism; France would be reentering some new community for European design and action. The Baltic areas could never be left out willingly. Wherever old and new martyrs' blood had reddened the soil beneath and around the desecrated sanctuaries of Christ, thither the redeeming rays of thought and plan and prayer must be directed.

It was in the summer of 1955 that a secretariat for World Council affairs was attached to the Bishop of Berlin's office, on the initiative of the Protestant Church Administration Board.[3] It had to deal largely with the problems of East and West integration and sought a useful contact with such constructive units as the *Information protestante*, a documentation service newly designed to cooperate with the Council of Europe in Strasbourg.

It was also in the late summer of that year that East Germany's ecumenical study groups were advised to be instrumental in making the church's oneness across the barriers of continents a living concern even in the smallest of parishes. For this purpose there was a nationwide distribution of the warm and wellworded prayers in Olive Wyon's admirable Quaker collection based on the Orthodox *Sobornost* and the French Father Paul Couturier's *Unity Octave*.[4]

Berlin, the meeting-ground of East and West, became a shelter and even a home for quite a few, and not the worst, among those engaged in holy experiments of atonement and regeneration. It was first of all through these regenerating people of prayer and service that light came into the long-forsaken city which in 1955 still had a monthly average of four abductions and political murders. No wonder that the city's spiritual leader came to feel how much more than a customary portion of care was committed to him just beyond the century's zenith. He knew for

---

[2] Come Over Into Macedonia: The Story of a Ten-Year Adventure by Harold B. Allen. Rutgers University Press.

[3] The Protestant Church Administration Board is an agency of the Church of Berlin and Brandenburg, which is a member church of the United Protestant Church, the major body in the EKiD.

[4] Praying for Unity by Olive Wyon. London, Edinburgh House, 1954.

certain he would be the last to cast off the committed burden of promise and pain. As he sought to set more time apart for contemplation and inward recreation, his physical health, weakened in the year of Evanston, improved astoundingly. Serenity and a renewed sense of forbearance made him an honest and frequent visitor to American and Soviet statesmen alike. Within one week, early in 1956, he sat in quiet talks with President Pieck of Pankow and Chancellor Adenauer of Bonn.

Christian lay people, even more than his clergy, admired his firm and balanced dealing when he set out to silence the over-agitated declarations and often vulgarly expressed outbursts of contending religious parties. Even in the danger zones of Central and East Germany, he did not favor his pastors and leading laymen dramatically assuming the martyr pose. In the winter of 1956, there were over sixty of his faithful languishing in isolation cells for church activities carried on in the eastern provinces.

Though he realized that there could be no European unity without a spiritual integrity and a practicable program, which was so long and badly missing, he did not shrink from calling listless and lighthearted those people of the western and southern hemispheres who readily assumed that "Europe was over the hump."

Though it be true that "the genius of creation once belonging to Europe alone,"⁵ is increasingly shared by two divergent continents, their concepts and ideas are not of their own, but coming to strange fruit in strange soil, as another American has rightly observed. Though Europe's primacy is a thing of the past, she is still a prodigious power, a ward of spiritual values and a safeguard against aggressive world materialism.

It was from Europe that the church and cultural mission went out to the non-Christian countries of Asia and to America. Christians from Europe have greatly contributed toward the present growth of the indigenous young churches in Asia.

⁵ *Fire in the Ashes*, Theodore H. White. William Sloane, New York, 1953. The quotations following are taken from Otto Dibelius' talk on the tenth anniversary of the churches' Commission on International Affairs. Cf. *Ecumenical Review*, Geneva, 1956, vol. 8, no. 4.

A great deal still remains to be done. The crucial factor which confronts the Christian churches with tasks they never had to face before is militant materialism which proclaims itself as the ideology of a great new future. A hopeful counteraction cannot be organized with material weapons. It will have to be undertaken by persons with a firm faith. These persons may all have their own confessional views. Yet they will not become an effective force until the confessional barriers are overcome and the divergencies of church form welded together by the one tremendous task which they have to face.

A divided Europe is doomed to decline. We must either have a United States of Europe or else Europe's cultural heritage will be a prey to others just as the noble accomplishments of the early Christians disappeared for a thousand years under the influence of the barbarians' great migration.

Now it would be fatal if the union of Europe were achieved on a purely materialistic basis. The God-given questions of man and mankind are the only ones which make life on earth worth while. The ultimate searchings of mind and soul must not be thrust aside as merely private affairs. More united spiritual leadership should be established between the nations and their churches, parallel with their economic union.

Europe came to birth under the cross. It is only under the cross that she will be able to survive.

These historic words were written when a leading Lutheran, O. Frederick Nolde and an equally prominent Anglican layman, Sir Kenneth Grubb, asked the Bishop to commemorate a decade's work of the churches' Commission on International Affairs. With the fervent hope that Europe and her culture might survive, the Bishop was still growing and preparing for his ministry of reconciliation. With a rising number of Christians in East and West, he shared the glorious vision of a world society in keeping with Christ's command and kingly promise. He was glad to learn from the Asian-born Christians a patience which was never passive, and, from such an indigenous Lutheran as Rajah B. Manikam, an optimism which was never illusory or irresponsible.[6] And indeed, the bishop of the long-divided German capital could stand some friendly prospect with rising hope for the years ahead.

Though many a European on the continent knew Otto Dibelius to be firm when firmness was the call of the hour, it is basically more truthful to remember that with the growing years, personal enmity became the one thing of which he himself became an enemy.

It was gratifying and new, like unexpected morning rays, when in the fall of 1955 a conspicuous group of non-German churchmen of the East came "to pay homage" in a significant response to the first trip the Bishop made after what the people of the East called the Evanston investiture. One of the British weeklies had the following report under the auspicious heading, "September, 1955—Reconciliation in Berlin":

With a delegation of eight churchmen representing the four major denominations of Czechoslovakia, Bishop Chabada of Bratislava arrived in the Soviet sector of Berlin for a two weeks' visit to East and West Germany. The visit, coming as a reply to the Bishop of Berlin's goodwill mission to Prague, signifies the mutual character of the new relations between churches that had been separated not only by the tension of East and West, but also by the extreme type of nationalism which had been rampant after Czechoslovakia's grave suffering from Nazi protectors who had tried to suppress the churches even in their own German lands. Outstanding among the confessing churchmen who survived the Nazi persecution is Otto Dibelius. His first foreign mission after his election as Joint President of the World Council was directed to Czechoslovakia.

To express the Czech's acknowledgment of Dr. Dibelius' act of reconciliation, the leader of the new delegation, Dean Hromadka of Prague University, handed over the episcopal cross, emblem of the last German church leader in Moravia, to the Bishop of Berlin.

---

[6] *Christianity and the Asian Revolution*, edited by Bishop R. B. Manikam. Madras and Bombay, 1954.

There followed a winter in which the Bishop was to enter even more deeply those parts of the earth in which the human soul attaches a magical reality and a strangely living hope to such ensigns as Moravia's ancient holy cross.

In the long winter of 1956, the aim of the world church spokesmen in action, and also in retreat, was New South Wales in Australia. Dibelius was requested to attend ecumenical meetings there as the European member of the World Council's presidium. Coming also was his co-president the Metropolitan of Malabar, whose church kept and honored some relics of St. Thomas, apostle of our Lord. It was significant for the churches' solidarity across the continents and their traditions that the successor of the martyred apostle, the bishop of a minority church, should join the spiritual leader of East Germany in carrying the burden and the transcendant dignity of the World Church's constituted leadership.

Both the Syrian Orthodox and the Protestant leader were agonized by the sad sights of India's displaced millions. Both of them wondered if the white missionary societies should not have given means of initiative to native Christians earlier than they actually did. Both of them deplored to what extent the Roman Catholic Church had caused acts of reprisal to be inflicted on her own clergy. Evidently the reports of the U. S. Navy Lt. Thomas A. Dooley on the happenings of Vietnam and Indo-China were historically correct.[7]

Australia, however, struck them as being more at a distance from Asia than she was in actual geography. For one thing, the southern continent was very British and very white. Furthermore, it was the hemisphere of wide and untouched stretches of farms, like the Victoria River Downs providing forty acres of grazing for each of the semi-wild cattle.

But deep in Dibelius' heart was suffering, writhing, and fermenting Asia. Would the white Australian churches awaken to the call audible from southern Indonesia, a call almost as urgent

---

[7] *Deliver Us From Evil*, by T. A. Dooley, Farrar, Straus, and Cudahy, 1956.

as the one that had come from Macedonia some 1900 years ago? There were some responsive pioneers of Christian unity and solidarity in the splendid cities of Southern Australia. With the exception of some unbalanced criticizing of American aid, Dibelius liked the constructive outline which Malcolm Mackay had given on behalf of the Australian Council of Churches:

It has been borne upon our thinking that some of the greatest danger points in the world situation today have received stimulation from Southeast Asia. It was the accent of the Bandung Conference for the Asian and African nations which brought colonialism and racialism to the forefront of international thinking.

Let us find the church's answer to want and hate in Southeast Asia. Now that China is no longer open to us and India and Pakistan are increasingly doubtful quantities in terms of Christian strategy, it is becoming apparent that a tremendous amount depends upon Australia and New Zealand.

We stand at the very threshold of developing relations between the Christians of Australia and the Indonesian churches. Manila has already given indications of its leadership with the projected Asian Council for Ecumenical Mission.

We believe that without a spiritual undertone any material aid program must inevitably fail. We are not unaware of the failure of the United States material aid given to China, without adequate responsibility in the field of ideas.

However, let us come together with a mind open to the developments of the future.

The churches' call to assemble in the southern hemisphere with an open mind made Berlin's bishop even more hopeful with regard to the reconciliation of the races converging in these meaningful parts of the earth. He regretted that, for reasons of illness, Dr. Menzies, political leader of Australia's Commonwealth and soon to be a visitor to Federal Germany's Chancellor, had to cancel his part in the reception at Canberra Parliament House. But he was glad to speak on "The Church and the Nations" in Sydney's Town and Assembly

Halls under the joint chairmanship of Alan Watson, the Presbyterian and R. B. Low, the President-General of Australia's
Methodist Church. Addressing the thriving people of Sydney,
he could not help remembering Albert Schweitzer's honest and
fair appeal to the Christ-given sense of sacrifice in order to
make interracial mission a truly ecumenical cause, enriched by
mutual sharing. These were his words:

*Blessed are those who establish ultimate values in advance, in
the surrounding of our struggling and agonizing world. Blessed
is each nation that inwardly returns to the foundation from
which it sprang, and to the task for which its proper place, its
culture, and its own resources have prepared it.*

*God made us, not we ourselves. In him we live and move
and have our being. No nation will ever forget this without
evoking harm and hardship on its own.*

*It is true that people today are learning more than in earlier
centuries. They are also performing more than ever before. They
are performing so much now that they can blow up and smash
the whole of the earth if they wish to. At the same time, they
become poorer in their essence of being. The capacity of con-
centrating their minds and thoughts decreases rapidly. No
longer do they produce works of art and culture which men will
admire and enjoy for centuries. Most of all, they are losing the
will to sacrifice. Millions say they admire Albert Schweitzer.
But these millions are by no means making up their minds to
help their suffering fellowmen of other races by sacrificing their
lives as Albert Schweitzer did. While wounds are still bleeding
and the misery of refugees is as great as ever, the number of
ambulance and nursing sisters is wholly inadequate. The number of pastors and priests steadily declines while the world's
population rapidly increases.*

*Let us, in earnest, beseech God that he may reinspire our
machine-ridden minds, our selfishly sophisticated beings with
a new faith resulting in springs of action like the blessed streams
of living water.*

On his long journey back to Europe, Berlin's Bishop viewed

both the scene of Southeast Asia and the Middle East with fuller knowledge and eyes more widely opened than they could have been at the outset of his Australian mission. In the five weeks between, his thought and action had virtually outgrown the project stated in the Australian Council's introductory letter, "to help form a spiritual counterpart" to Asia's equivalent of the Marshall Plan. The actual issues stated and clarified in Sydney, Canberra, and Gilbulla had made it desperately obvious that the attuning of some "spiritual undertone of the Colombo Plan" would be an undertaking blatantly incapable of honoring the God revealed in Christ, near as a Judge and Preserver to every race and nation alike.

A year earlier, no one in Europe had heard about the city of Bandung. Now, however, the European President of the World Council of Churches returned from a distant hemisphere with more than just a journalistic headline claim associated with that place in Indonesia. European newspapers had rightly welcomed the Ceylonese Sir John Kotelawa's warning lest the Bandung talks should lull the transatlantic critics of "old-fashioned colonialism" into ignoring the subtle and, in effect, much more enslaving methods of the modern totalitarian state expanding from the largest and most monolithic of this century's empires.

Nine months later, Dibelius was in a position to realize that there evolved from the Bandung resolutions still greater issues. As he evaluated those resolutions of 1955, he felt the World Council of Churches would not be a world institution if its leaders did not take Asia's new plans and projects into active consideration. It was high time, he felt, that church leaders should direct their thoughts to a global strategy in which the Christian minority could have a good conscience. The talk of Christian majorities and Christian states was for him a thing of the past.

In the factual appraisal of the Asian-African development he followed again a report of his younger associate in Evanston, Charles H. Malik of Beirut, Lebanon. Dibelius deemed the questions raised in Malik's Evanston Mars Lecture a challenge worth recalling and presenting to Europe and the East;

How systematically will Asia continue to be racially estranged and embittered from Australia, America, and Western Europe?

What will be Asia's concept of freedom? The Bandung debates has ushered in the issue whether freedom is only national freedom, the freedom of a group, or a race vis-a-vis other groups and races, or whether the meaning of freedom in the individual human soul is not the primary and most important meaning. How much do Asia and Africa understand and value this original personal freedom? Here we are face to face with the deepest issue in the world, the issue of the being and destiny of man's individual soul.

How far is communism already advanced throughout Asia, advanced in frightening, in overawing, in undermining people?[8]

As he traversed the largest of all continents, Berlin's bishop felt a deep solidarity. He desired to do justice to each part of Asia, most especially to the Near and Middle East where he was bound to stay a little longer now. He had been to Israel and Egypt in quieter times.

In view of the present anti-colonial tide, he would ask rather topical questions, again in the words of the Lebanese spokesman: How far advanced is the communist softening-up process upon the Asian and African mind? Is there a notable distinction, in this context, between the heartland of Asia, namely, China and India, and the periphery of Asia, namely, countries like Ceylon and the Philippines, Iran and Iraq, Israel and Lebanon, Syria and Turkey?

---

[8] The Problem of Coexistence by C. H. Malik, pp. 12 ff. Evanston, 1955. Northwestern University Press.

CHAPTER TWENTY-ONE

Unto Whom
Much Is Given

In 1956, the Republic of Turkey was most instructive, illustrative and explosive. She had vegetated for some decades as a secular state pretending to be no longer interested in the religion of Islam, but neutral in the most enlightened and sober sense of the word.

Now, however, Istanbul and her coastal areas were the scene of violent attacks on innocent priests. A great number of Orthodox churches and chapels were being destroyed by mobs of people carried away by the dream of an all-Arabian empire. Orthodox priests were not permitted by the Turkish government to appear in public vested in the robes which Orthodox tradition and ecclesiastical law prescribed for all of them. The Ecumenical Patriarch of Constantinople was deeply grateful for the visit Dibelius paid to him and for the expression of the World Council's sympathy conveyed on that moving occasion. But never could the Patriarch leave his residence. Further persecution and violence were in the air. Traditional Islamic fanatics and neo-pagan secularists joined hands in order to eliminate Christian ethics and culture.

If Nasser of Egypt could get rid of a Christian soldier like Sir Glubb Pasha overnight, why should Allah's sons on Asia's outpost tolerate a church whose leaders had themselves lowered their peaceful masks? Was it not a colleague and friend of Istanbul's American-trained Patriarch who had the effrontery to proclaim that the Turks should be deprived of the titles and professional rights which the British Crown had conceded to them throughout the first half of the century? Was this a church worthy of the Christian name, which taught that Orthodox bishops could not err?

Dibelius had to listen to a still more burning question. Was a church with a world renown, a religious body united on the co-initiative of the Anglo-Saxon denominations, justified in keeping away from the scene where an archbishop incited extreme nationalism and refused to disown notorious terrorists? The place of terror of which everyone spoke since the fall of 1955 was the island of Cyprus, to which Paul had brought the gospel in its early purity. The source of the recent agitation was the movement for *enosis* or reunion with the Greek kingdom.

Dibelius remembered the first *enosis* revolt of the century. It failed because of the Greek government's loyalty to the international treaty of 1878 which granted British sovereignty on the island in exchange for British help in Turkey's struggle against Russia. Two Cypriot bishops were deported to Britain in 1931.

Some twenty years later, the revival of *enosis* was graver and of more international repercussion. A Cypriot bomb exploded in the Turkish Consulate at Salonika, ancient capital of Macedonia. The acts of retaliation against the Greek Orthodox of Istanbul, Ankara, and Ismir never seemed to end.

Yet Dibelius was told that the Communist International would deplore any future action taken against an intellectual who, in his robes of immunity, did all he could to make the existing together of Turks and Cypriots an impossibility. The island's spiritual, cultural, and political leader was Makarios, "the Blessed." He had just received a letter from Dibelius' honored friend, Archbishop Fisher of Canterbury, entreating him to denounce the acts of terror. The Cypriot leader had written back:

I am sincerely afraid that an official condemnation of events by myself . . . would involve a risk of exposing me rather unprofitably.

No wonder that the Russians came to love and honor this archbishop. He had been to Bandung. And surely the Bandung Conference was not only the birth, but also the dedication and spiritual activation of the Asian-African vision and purpose. The purpose was anticolonialism, that eastern drive to be followed by the blood-letting of gouty Mother Europe and, finally, by an extermination of all the Anglo-Saxon commonwealths and states.

By this time Dibelius had some experience of Orthodox church leaders in the Near and Middle East. He never felt entitled to examine British and American policies as to their possible faults in earlier periods. But he knew that in the minds of the modern Greeks, the church and the communist party were the only institutions which carried any conviction. He well remembered Damaskinos', the kingmaker's, brave resistance to Nazi intruders in Greece. At that time, the British were on the side of the church and on the side of liberty. In Cyprus, it was now, to all appearances, the other way round; the Communists were on the side of the church and, with some surprising pretext, on the side of liberty. Even American public opinion was so beguiled that some of its leaders did not seem to know which side they should favor now.

When Athens' Archbishop collapsed and died in the middle of that awful swinging circle, Dibelius wrote to the Greek Holy Synod words of sympathy, sorrow, and warning alike.[1] He had sufficient proof that the Greek Church had acted in a maturer and more propitious way under Damaskinos than she was doing now under the influence of Makarios. Dibelius, therefore,

---

[1] First telegram from Bishop Otto Dibelius (March 22, 1956) to the Holy Synod of the Greek Orthodox Church on the sudden death of Archbishop Spiridos of Athens.

did not follow the Roman contention that "a more representative assortment of the believers in violence than just some rebellious priest should have been deported" from Cyprus. He was ready to acknowledge that Makarios was approaching, in a militant and rather unblessed way, the reputation of the Middle East's hero helping to overthrow the whole of western tradition and culture.

Perhaps it was true that the cultural leaders of the West should have reckoned long before with God's judgment in history. However, no leader of the reborn Protestant Church was willing to dispense with Christ's sayings even in the more and more complicated fabric of modern world movements. The kingship of Christ was not to be obscured behind the worldly totalitarian issues demanding man's ardent loyalty in the Middle East and elsewhere:

The ethic of Christianity is valid in all situations of life, or it has no value at all. "Unto whomsoever much is given, of him shall much be required, and to whom men have committed much, of him they will ask the more" (Luke 12:48).

German Protestants had learned their lesson under the rule of strange prophets advocating world salvation by the blood of one race alone. They could not help finding some similarities between Teutonic deeds of justification by race and the more aggressive acts of Panhellenic renaissance in the Cypriot movement for *enosis.*

Taking their lesson of the first half of the century seriously, German Protestants found some of Rome's predictions misleading with respect to the Middle East's issue between the old colonial and the new totalitarian powers of the world. One of the Rome-inspired predictions had it that the British government was frantically disabling itself. No British spokesman should be trusted if he mentioned the issue of religious liberty when bargaining over the terms of Soviet-British coexistence in the pending negotiations with Russia's leading Communists, now "bowing to kiss the hand of a British Queen."

The element of sophistry shone forth still more flimsily when

Catholic journalists set out to dissuade her Britannic Majesty's government, and with it the Church of England, from pleading the case of a man like Beran, the abducted leader of Prague, whom Berlin's bishop had in his mind when, in Czechoslovakia less than a year before, he discussed the prospect of a peacefully united Europe.

The astonishing piece of journalism which occupied the minds of many Christians on the continent went on with the following statement:

It had been hoped by some that the Soviet leaders might be made to understand that they would be much more favorably regarded in the western world if they allowed a greater measure of freedom in Central Europe, including religious freedom. But it will be of little use for the British side to raise the question of the banished Polish Cardinal or the abducted Archbishop of Prague. Whatever the British spokesmen may say, they can hardly say that they do not approve of banishing bishops.

It is not difficult, indeed, to imagine N. Khrushchev who is not without experience in these matters, giving his own friendly advice in Downing Street. "We've found it a mistake," he will say; "we've learned the hard way; we've found it bad policy. Now we are setting the bishops free, or pretending to, just when you are beginning to lock them up."

The Russians will give sardonic laughs when they hear about the bundles of incriminating documents found in the Archbishop's residence; about the bombs and armaments conveniently discovered in ecclesiastical buildings. They too, they will say, were in no way persecuting religion; they too were only removing prelates with whose persons an intolerable degree of national sentiment was popularly associated. Fine distinctions in personal conduct or theological allegiance will not seem to the Russians relevant. Whether they say it or not, they will believe that Britain has committed in Cyprus what they themselves have painfully learned to be a grave mistake.[2]

---

[2] *The Tablet*, London, 1956, vol. 207, no. 6043.

Christian people in Europe also became painfully aware that America's Protestant churches were eagerly subscribing to what Romeward-orientated diplomats ably translated from the *Osservatore Romano's* idiom into American English. Having been a long-time research student of diplomatic usages and evasive wordings, Berlin's Bishop knew very well that the predigested anti-papal sort of history was ever the easiest to write and to swallow in the western world.

As he had reconciled his sense of the historic with the essence of the Church Universal, so he also came to apply to the larger units what at first he had related to individual beings:

We must love men as they are, and not wait until they change into what we want them to be.

Dibelius has never denied his love for the man who was, in 1956 and long before, the sacred head of that imposing structure, the Church of Rome. When he traveled via Northern Africa and the greater part of Asia to Southwest Australia, Rome was his only stop between Berlin and Cairo. He arrived in Rome on January 21, 1956. Ten days before, Berlin's and all East Germany's Travelers Aid Organization had been disintegrated by Soviet German police. Among the arrested social workers of that organization most were Protestants. But the organization had Catholic associates who had helped the eastern refugees just as sympathetically, with an exceptional sense of solidarity and loyalty to the organization's Protestant leadership.

Hardly less than a million displaced and exiled persons had been succored by the missionaries on the track and in the railroad station on the zonal border. Their self-effacing work had been the Bishop of Berlin's constant source of satisfaction. But then it was no wonder that the Bishop of Rome was sharing in the prayerful good wishes for those outdoor Christians engaged in the mission to the destitute, the disowned, and the people discomforted by the restraining methods of Marxist materialism. Could he see the Protestant Bishop of Berlin right away? That was Pope Pius' question, raised spontaneously, voiced convincingly, but forwarded, alas, through the channels of Vatican and Federal diplomacy.

Though always paying his due respects, Otto Dibelius never really liked traditional diplomacy too deeply. For all his love of the Christian in this Pope, he was careful to point out that what was termed an audience, was out of the question. No formal addresses were exchanged. Pressmen and photographers were sent away. The Bishop was happy to notice how greatly interested the Pope was in Germany's eastern parts and in her pending reunification. However tense the Roman atmosphere was before and after that memorable day, the visit itself was happy and fruitful. As it was the first time since the Reformation that a leading Protestant went in that direction, it was not unlikely to become a landmark on the road to Europe's inner peace and integrity; it was one of the new incidents which the *Christian Century* rightly termed victories over the vast and terrible impersonalities which put the world at diplomatic or military stalemate; it indicated a sudden recognition of the fact that international politics was becoming an "I-thou matter."

All through the conversation, the Pope's voice was gentle and low. He was gracious, serene, and affable to this visitor—one in a hundred thousand—who did not bow to kiss His Holiness' hand. In its personal aspect, this was almost like a reunion of two Berliners recalling many seeds of sorrow and hope sown together in the prewar years. At that time when Pius XII was known as Eugenio Pacelli, Dean of Berlin's Diplomatic Corps, the German capital had a stature almost equaling that of 1956 when Berlin was western civilization's most important outpost within the steadily advancing eastern orbit.

The old Europe had been reduced to smaller dimensions outwardly. But neither the head of the Roman communion nor the Protestant leader of Berlin felt inwardly discouraged. A new Europe was bound to come. The spirit of a new day was already manifest in East and West. And though the Pope did not like to enter into talks on the ecumenical movement, the European continent's representative was straight on his way to

a new gathering in the active service of Christian unity. His
witness before and after Evanston was more and more appreciated as an "evidence that a united church might also become
a uniting church" living up to the promise of its common Lord
in faithful obedience.

The secular press and broadcast unanimously talked of "reunion schemes elaborated by the two top leaders among ecclesiastical statesmen!" Dibelius and Pacelli shared quite different
feelings when parting after twenty-two minutes of very private
communication. Both of them issued demurrers over the irresponsible reactions by the papers, so avidly read for their
money-making distortions. There were sensationalists, however,
not only in the press pools, but also much nearer to the respective sanctuaries, Catholic and Protestant. There were the
totalitarians among the Roman hierarchy on more than one
continent. Reviewing his fraternal visit, Dibelius was more
than ever convinced that Pius XII did not side with them.

The Pope seemed to bear no grudge toward Germany's leading Protestant for having long pleaded the case of the Paris
priest-workers recently divested of their commission.[3] Nor did
he ever deny him the right to denounce the Royal Spanish
decrees against the only seminar which Protestants upheld in
that country ruled by Fascists with the hierarchs' tacit approval.
Pacelli had known Dibelius long enough to realize whence he
came in the past and, more meaningful still, whither he was
going. With no remark whatsoever did he suggest a slowing up
of the Protestant's speed as he proceeded to that Australian
world meeting which was likely to draw all Christendom's attention to the atrocities inflicted by a Roman majority on a
weakened Protestant minority in Columbia.

Since Dibelius had sufficient proof that Pacelli was not personally interested in the totalitarian trends so repeatedly disfig-

---

[3] Otto Dibelius' plea for the French priest-workers in the sermon
preached at St. Mary's, East Berlin, March 7, 1954; for the Protestants of
Spain in the sermon preached at St. Mary's, June 7, 1955, and in a letter
of protest addressed to Dr. Joseph Frings, Cardinal-Archbishop of Cologne,
dated Berlin May 18, 1956.

uring the structure of the church, why should he have turned to other representatives of that disputed "denomination"? More than once and long before Berlin's bishop became one of the Presidents of the World Council, the Holy See had been invited to cooperate with the Council's committees for ecumenical action.

The world was not accustomed to take official utterings of the church too seriously. Only now Dibelius succeeded in making it clear to friend and foe alike that an invitation given in the name of Jesus Christ, is meant to be a genuine approach toward mutual sharing of historic gifts and earthly responsibilities. His whole visit was an endorsement of sincerity in a daring approach.

If love and charity were not to seek their own, if Christians of all creeds were bound to love their neighbors "as they are," why should the ordering of the Roman household be left primarily to the primitive or to the subtle among the authoritarians? Was not the Roman outcry in favor of the militant priestly rule on Cyprus painful enough with its astounding similarity to what the Soviet pressmen had to promulgate about the provocative acts of Great Britain? Who could deny that those very acts were fearfully dramatized because they might help the Russians to kill the Atlantic Treaty Organization after the European Defense Community had been undercut already?

Berlin's bishop had not been in the Middle East for nothing. If America's public opinion was partly to follow the anti-British and consequently the more authoritarian line in this respect, he had little to say to that. But when the whole episcopate of a Soviet satellite state was put in armor to "fight for the World Church's constitution" over against an "unruly President's unpardonable deviation," it only helped to clarify what a leader of a movement for Christian unity is and what he never should become.

Among the several Soviet-supported ecclesiastics who shouted out their well-rehearsed disgust was Lajos Vetö, "Lutheran" Bishop of Budapest and President of Hungary's Synod. These were his words:

The faithful of Hungary have requested us to invoke the message and resolutions of the World Council's second Assembly held in Evanston less than two years ago.

We consider the message and the resolutions to be binding for Bishop Dibelius, the elected representative of our continent's churches in the presidium of the World Council.

The Council's executive committee should examine closely what kind of bargain Bishop Dibelius intended to strike when he undertook this unprecedented step into the secret chamber of the most enigmatic of archpriests. We will expect an early explanation from the Executive and a subsequent proclamation of the present or a newly formed presidium.

The Bishop of Debrecen went even further in pointing out that Otto Dibelius was backing up the warmongers who increasingly threatened the youthful Soviet German Republic:

Through the political act of his Vatican visit, Bishop Dibelius has greatly endangered the oneness of the Protestant Church in both the Germanies.

Vetö and all his Hungarian colleagues, "Lutheran and Calvinist," had to wait on their episcopal bench until, more than six months later, Otto Dibelius, still being very much in the World Council's presidium, was due to attend the Council's central committee meeting at a place not far from Lajos Vetö's Budapest and Janos Peter's Debrecen.

At the person-to-person encounter, nothing was heard any longer of charges uttered by Peter such as "backing up the warmongers." It was only a month since Dibelius had signed an appeal of sixty-two German synod representatives against one-sided measures of rearmament and conscription. At Germany's 1956 synod, he also proved to be the immutable guardian of Protestant unity overcoming ecclesiastical lines of division as well as political barriers and zonal blockades. He would never grow tired of appealing, with fatherly passion, to the traditional Lutherans and the keen "confessing" brothers alike:

Christ is not divided. Truth cannot be divided either. Nor can truth be divorced from charity and human reality. The cold-hearted way in which some of our intellectuals divorce a God-given inheritance from the day-to-day decisions and adjustments has no place with the spirit of the new day.

The church's oneness is full of life's manifold treasures, joined together in the harmony of a new creation. This harmony is essentially different from the homogeneity advocated by the protagonists of automatism. Outwardly, our church may be as poor as she is young in her experience of oneness. Yet she is never again to become a mere milestone at the side of the broad way along which quite a number of nations are passing on a spurious and visionless march toward complete animalic uniformity.

Somehow this voice from an inward realm, from an independent sphere of life was bursting forth to penetrate the orbit of monolithic uniformity. Coming to Hungary in midsummer 1956, Dibelius met his colleague of Budapest who had been incited to "expect any early explanation" about certain "bargains." Again the person-to-person encounter superseded all bargaining, all reasoning, all formal explaining. Silently the two servants of Christ shook hands and felt the loving forgiveness of their Lord warming their hearts with mutuality. It was in a brotherly spirit that this Bishop of Budapest accompanied Dibelius up into the Matra Mountains and acted as an interpreter when Berlin's bishop preached to a multitude of peasants and townspeople in the ancient church of Myregyhaza. His text was Christ's last saying to his disciples gathered on the fortieth day after Easter: "All authority in heaven and on earth has been given to me" (Matthew 28:18). It was no easy sermon to translate for one of those church leaders of whom local pastors in other parishes said: "They are installed in order to watch lest we obey God rather than men."

The Sunday worship with the staunch and sturdy peasants of the Matra Mountains was an auspicious introduction to the important gathering at which Dibelius shared responsibility with two other members of the World Council's presidium, America's Henry Knox Sherrill and Scotland's John Baillie. It was the first meeting which the Council's central committee held within the Soviet orbit. The place was a workers' Reintegration Center named Galyatetö. Property of the Communist-controlled Trade Union (no other union exists in Hungary) the spacious tavern provided a unique background for an interdenominational body's findings on "The Building of a Responsible International Order." In the lively discussions, two contributions were particularly reassuring as to the maintenance of the fundamental truths so often infringed on where totalitarian ideologies prevail. One of the spirited reaffirmations came from the World Council's General Secretary Visser t'Hooft: "By the acceptance of the invitation to hold its annual meeting in Hungary, the World Council showed once again that it lives its own life in complete independence from any particular political system or ideology and desires to render its witness in all parts of the world." Another good word which the Bishop welcomed with a deep and passionate concern came from Princeton's John Mackay: "It is a scandalous way in which the cold war of our days obscures truth and the necessity for free relations between people. The Christian Church cannot accept dictates from any government regarding contacts between Christians wherever they may be."

Hungarians and others in the Soviet orbit had been taught to praise loudly the progressive kind of life which people were attaining collectively wherever the doctrines of Marx and Lenin were accepted as the dogma of state religion. Now it was Dibelius' turn to point out that the reputedly progressive doctrinaires were not devoting themselves sufficiently to the complex problems of refugees and displaced persons:

In the old days when countries were conquered, people were simply killed. Then came the time when whole populations were brought under control. The solution of the so-called progressive era has been to expel people. The refugee problem is acute in India and Palestine as well as in Germany. The persons, the human beings involved in that problem are often dealt with by barbarian concepts utterly incompatible with a Christian sense of responsibility. But what is the use of worries and indictments behind our closed doors? Let all our member churches rise to demonstrate that they, like us, through the guidance of Christ, have become rather unlike this world's eternal pharisees who worry professionally about the state of the earth, washing their hands in vain. Let us, in all due solidarity, proclaim to East and West alike what ought to be said in view of the deadening danger surrounding all of us physically, morally, and spiritually.

The World Council's central committee elected a group of three to draft a statement to be read in every congregation of the 165 member churches on all five continents. The three men were Otto Dibelius, W. A. Visser t'Hooft, and Charles P. Taft of America's Protestant Episcopal Church. Unanimously their draft resolution was adopted, and a fine spirit prevailed to the end of that meeting in Hungary. It was especially gratifying to witness the unfailing devotion and self-effacing cooperation of the American Colonel Francis Pickens Miller, supporter of the Bishop for nearly thirty years and life-saver of another great German.

A week later, Dibelius was addressing the huge Kirchentag rally in Frankfurt on the Main. Over a thousand had come there from the Anglo-Saxon world to join nearly half a million lay people in a world witness of faith and hope and love. Hymns of joy and thanksgiving, in German and English, were sung after the Bishop's reading of these words from the World Council's statement adopted in Hungary the week before:

To move out of a state of cold war into one of real peace requires respect for truth under all circumstances. People must not be subjected to deliberate misrepresentation and false propaganda. They must have access to information and be free to discover the truth for themselves. People must be free to travel, to meet and to know their neighbors, through personal encounter to seek understanding and create friendship, and thus to achieve mutual confidence and respect. They must also be free to choose by whom and in what way they wish to be governed. They must be free to obey the dictates of their consciences. They must be free to worship God, to witness to their faith and to have their children educated in it in church, school or youth meeting. We call upon all Christians to lay these matters to heart and to seek these ends in a spirit of prayer and of penitence for past failures and in the name of their Lord and Master, who is the Way, the Truth, and the Life.

CHAPTER TWENTY-TWO

No Pilgrim's Regress

EARLY IN THE twentieth century, a Catholic journalist of some international reputation made the oft-repeated statement that the history of Christendom in modern Europe was largely a story of lost balance. Believing in the ultimate triumph of a planned world society, the Catholic observer regretted only one tragic consequence of the Reformation: the leaders of Christendom in the sixteenth century began to lose their wonted interest in outward planning just as they abandoned their trusteeship for dealing with the souls of men. The dominion over man's conscience, thought, and will was left to the more worldly organs of community life. After the French Revolution the nineteenth century's agnostics succeeded in replacing all spiritual authority by temporal expediency and materialistic accumulation of power.

While the modern state rose to unlimited heights of power and compulsion, the lack of balance and the temporal weakness of the Christian Church became obvious indeed. Yet as the twentieth century advanced it also became clear that human planning is doomed to final failure if it does not start with and grow from the divine origin of human life. They seemed to be few in number and weak in influence who joined together in order to proclaim that man's true destiny is never attained through a drive for human autonomy. Yet their testimony, running against the grain of popular thought, continued: man's true destiny was infinitely more than material welfare and operational efficiency.

The hunger and thirst after righteousness was reasserted as being what it had been from the beginning of creation, a hunger and thirst of the soul. In her solidarity with the hungry and thirsty of a machine-ridden age, the Church of Christ regained some of the balance she required in order to assume her proper place in mankind's history. Her rightful place was shown to be below the pedestal of man's self-glorification, but also high above the pattern of collective impersonal planning.

The few pilgrims who have been bold enough to hold, over against the frightening background of our crowded cities' failures and frustrations, that every person is made in the image of God, have made their lives begin afresh from foundations long hidden underneath a cover of dust and embers. Therefore the inner warmth and radiance of their lives shine forth like watch fires through the night, promising every child of God glorious liberty with the morrow's dawn.

The Europe of the "enlightened" French Revolution and the brave promise of nineteenth century progress lost their world renown in the first half of the twentieth century. In the same war-haunted period, however, the Church Universal was roused to dig deep in order to unearth those hidden foundations of hers, the New Man born to be free and destined to survive through sacrificial love, through sharing with the hungry and thirsty God's gracious and bountiful gifts.

In the heart of Europe almost all of one man's lifetime was offered to make the twentieth century approach willingly this task of recreating and sharing. It took a lonely watchman's nightly prayer, a fervent preacher's quiet meditation, a richly endowed man's fragrant offering and blameless sacrifice to make mankind aware that there is nowhere a region in which Christ would not continue to exert his healing power.

However splendidly the previous century seemed to have

ended, the young candidate for Prussia's state-church splendor felt called upon early to stand out against an agnostic school of thought. As he painfully listened to the voices of the agnostics, indulging in elaborate pleadings of what they labeled "a post-Christian era," he knew they were the voices of hirelings. To him, however, Christ's real presence was beyond the range of speculation.

Only through a determined pilgrim's faithful renouncing of personal prestige and expediency was he able to give the generation growing nearer to the end of history a new and quickening lease on life. This man, graced and privileged to become a partner in the making of history, may have to wait a long time until the rightful historian rises to do justice to his endowment and to pass on his legacy to followers and friends alike.

When he was young, the man born to be free turned his back on the pomp and pageantry possessing the life of his native capital city. He chose the town of Wittenberg, once the cradle of Europe's Reformation, for leading the growing generation into a movement for life-reform and life-sharing. Here the vices of a decadent aristocracy had little influence over young men's souls.

From Luther's Wittenberg he followed the call of his early fathers. Tilling the eastern soil, they had wrought with one hand at the plough while the other held a weapon to show the mighty intruders that all sacred life is commitment.

All commitment is sacrifice—the young pilgrim found this written on the yellowed parchments of inherited chronicles, and on the tombstones whose gilded letters shone forth as he trod along the grassy footpaths near the ancient sanctuaries built of unhewn rock. Here in the land of venture and youthful endeavor, every little thing mattered. Here in the frontier area, ancient folk songs were sung like sacred hymns. Here Christian charity was unpretentious and genuine. "One loving heart set another on fire." Prayers were uttered in primeval fervency. Art was as colorful as it was simple. Garments were befitting and beautiful. In the borderland there was indeed an unchecked potential of true humanity. The true partaker of the frontier life, the pastor, the pilgrim, the pioneer was never to relieve himself of the pledge indelibly carved into the wood and stone of Eastern Protestant Germany.

All commitment is sacrifice, and so is love. Wandering in freedom, eagerly in search of fortune wherever fortune would prove to be a potent gift of heaven, the man of Luther's Wittenberg came to love and cherish the culture of Britain, most of all the lowlands of Scotland. The year he spent in the quiet cottage on the wind-swept banks of the Firth of Forth was also the year in which he became convinced of the reality of a new realm. Henceforth no storm, no lulling influence of lust or leisure could ever take away the sense of nearness of a better land. With John Mott and William Temple, he was to sing of the city of God:

> How gleam thy watch fires through the night
> With never-fainting ray!
> How rise thy towers, serene and bright!
> To meet the dawning day!
> In vain the surge's angry shock,
> In vain the drifting sands;
> Unharmed upon the eternal rock
> The eternal city stands.

Empires collapsed. Millions of deceived human beings were immolated for earthly ends. Berlin, in the first world war already a fallen city, called him back from the East. The call implied the paramount task of reaffirming that God himself was in the midst of an island city destined to rise unharmed out of the roaring and troubled waters.

When the victorious powers, the world's Big Four for a time, decreed that Europe's heart should be dismembered; when the sophisticated of his compatriots buried their guilt in derision and self-abandonment, the Holy Fount preacher won a wholly different victory by being just himself, remaining a humble child of God. He was not ashamed to hold up before God his fatherly saying that nowhere should his children cease to seek his face for wisdom and guidance in overcoming the will of the adversaries.

Evasive agnostics of the enlightened era talked millions of listeners into the fatal belief that the new assessment of man as only one of the earth-engendered mammals would not spread widely over Europe. Subjectivism and relativism became the slogans of the intellectuals who were so fashionable in the years following the first world war.

When the "intrinsic goodness of democratic man" ushered in a more violent antagonism against the scriptural concept of man's life and value under God, it was a fact of historic consequence that the man who preached to the bewildered masses of Berlin felt he could not breathe in the subjectivist atmosphere of the uncommitted mind. What he felt for himself, he was ready to proclaim to all who would hear him:

The keys of our personal existence are not ours alone. God made the keys, not we ourselves. Our fathers in faith helped in their making. We can still rely on the life witness of our fathers to a great extent. Filled with gratitude, with warm remembrance, and with loving children's unfailing reverence, we hand over the keys of our personal conviction willingly to the church of our fathers. Even for our cultural life, we rejoice in an inheritance which is imperishable, unfading, and undefiled.

The guardian of everything beautiful and sacramental in human life felt more than an emotional urge to get Christians of all continents to rise to the rapidly changing world situation. If it was his birthright to discern the signs of the times, he was surely entitled to discuss with any brother in Christ how far the world's increasing denial of the human person, of his unique inheritance, was speeding enormous masses along the road to the predicted world-wide revolution.

Being himself a child of the East, an heir of early Christian servants to the East, and a watchman on guard at the eastern window in the wall of his entrusted citadel, he built a bridge toward the West. When the bridge was open, he widened it. When it was wide enough, he helped to fortify it. How many in the East had asked him if the bridge would endure the on-coming tide of violence, hatred, and lust!

To America he was invited more often than he could go. Re-turning enriched from each crossing, he felt a concern for Europe and the East deeper than ever. His competent steward-ship, always acting on the living situation, came to include the Christian minorities of India and Southeast Asia. It was a pilgrim's steady advance, a climbing of untrodden paths. Whenever there was a venturesome thing to be done for the cause of Christian liberty, he was there to follow the vision, and he would not settle down until every perspective was explored. There were intervals for fasting, prayer, and meditation. But seldom if ever did he relax. Admiring the simple and genuine witness in the writings of John Bunyan, he often said: "There is indeed no pilgrim's regress."

Not that he looked at leisure in a negative way. For him leisure and creative art were intimately related:

He is a poor man who has no time to enjoy the treasures of our inherited music. Indeed I would hardly call him a man who cannot join in the simple songs of our children.

No matter how wilfully and badly God's image was distorted in the repellent varieties of appearance and fashion, God re-mained to him "the First, the only Fair." His triumph with the risen Christ and the New Man made beauty shine forth as an aspect of "reality seen with the eyes of love." It was in this context that he often recalled what he had learned within the fellowship of the Anglican Cowley Fathers who received him early as a guest and a brother.

He always remained a realist, sober, detached, and seldom carried away by his emotional response. But in the utilitarian modern setting he maintained the glorious fact that there is no fruitful issue of life where reality, beauty, and charity are kept apart. To him the three were essentially interdependent. He would not judge the products of art by the crude question as to whether man's desultory and much distorted self would de-sire to live with them for awhile. His real test was rather the extent to which pieces of art were making an image of God's fatherly perfection.

Always in search of a genuine motive in art and handicraft, he derived deep satisfaction from the fact that the appeal of mankind's creative and re-creative instinct was different with each person. Within the scope of a person's endowment, that appeal could mean an enduring enrichment of life. But then it seemed to him important that a real person should neither permit himself nor encourage those living in communion with him to divorce charity and beauty from the working-day's reality. The craftwork and the paintings which came to adorn the lovely Faraday Wayside Hall when it became the episcopal residence were the same pieces which kept him company when the Nazi government addressed him as a disfrocked pastor, when he had to live over a garage and subsequently in a damp basement whither the dignified and the aesthetic were proudly reluctant to come.

He was not likely ever to forget that great decisions were often made in little and narrow surroundings. His various periods of isolation and imprisonment had only deepened the meaning of forsakenness and pain. The nearer the goal, the harder the going. There was no pilgrim's regress. The gate was narrow and the way was hard that would lead to life.

His deepened sense of the mystical and eucharistic element in the sacred and yet unrenowned parts of the world, made the pilgrim mindful of places where Christian history was made. His gift of bringing back to life an almost forgotten past was often contagious and a source of inspiration to many.

The footpath from Cavala to Philippi where St. Paul came over into Macedonia . . . the Devonshire village of Crediton where St. Boniface heard the call to bring the gospel of Christ over into Germany . . . the Baltic hill of Tannenberg where, on Easter Sunday, 1410, the Knights in Order won the decisive victory over the barbarian tribes of the Slavs . . . the Saxon enclosure of Breitenfeld where Gustavus Adolphus, King of Sweden, gave his life to save the Protestant religion for the whole continent . . . Edinburgh's churchyard of the Grey-

friars where a whole nation took a solemn vow in holy covenant with God . . . and William Penn's Philadelphia, the city
of a holy enterprise surrounding America's Hall of Independence—no one could ever hear him speak of these places and
go away with the thought that it is the stately and fashionable
features of history which matter in the end. All historic events
turn upon the hinges of individual persons:

*To understand God's history with men is to relive the de-
cisions of those who made their choice with him. The story of
men's self-glorification is a succession of broken shrines. History, however, seen with Christ, is a wondrous evolution of
healing and sharing. Without the spirit of healing and sharing,
there is no integration. Without our sacrificial love, there is
no hearing of the call sent forth to the fellow-laborers with
God.*

The preacher's times of testing were after the second world
war. Four Big Powers came to govern and re-educate his fallen
nation. It did not seem to be an item of their united program
to have newborn children of that nation ever welcomed again.

The number of illegitimate unions rose fantastically as "free
love" was propagated in the four zones of Germany. A host of
doctors, surgeons, nurses, and half-trained operational assist-
ants were set in motion to continue the process of killing which
had dealt with the grown-up species of man.

When fewer and fewer women dared to apply for clothing
and temporary accommodation where a living child could be
born, Berlin's bishop, now chairman of all East Germany's
church leaders' conference, opened an unexpectedly great number of well-equipped clinic retreats. And this was the letter he
sent out to hundreds of thousands of German women:

*Yours may be the temptation to have the grandest and most
precious gift of growing life destroyed by intrusion into a sacred
vessel, your body, created in the heavenly image. We will now
help you to overcome the all-surrounding temptation in a joyful triumph and victory.*

With her Home Mission re-equipped and ready for the task, the Church of Berlin and Brandenburg is offering succor and safety to each newborn child whose parents cannot, for stated reasons of emergency, afford maintenance.

I warmly appeal to all of you young mothers: Rise up from the common ground of annihilation! Ponder and treasure in your hearts that which is your church's great message during this testing time, in your very own situation.

For your decision, I entreat you to accept my words of encouragement in the same spirit in which they have grown in a fatherly heart. I have seen to it that loving hands are waiting to give all that human sympathy and help can gladly give to any child—maybe your child.

I also implore you: In setting your face to the oncoming hour of God's design, be ye quiet in spirit. At the same time, be joyous as you anticipate the coming into our world of what has presently entered into a God-willed process of achieving the greatest of all realities, a wholesome human life. The very real love of the Creator is waiting to embrace your child.

The warm and outgoing appeal was more than a forbearing gesture. It was a revolution, and one need not enter into statistics in order to demonstrate how the turning points in history are the fruits of faith and hope and a personal love which seeks not its own.

Just as the pilgrim took along all these wayward women of the road, so he also did everything to relieve them of social timidity. For those responsible for counseling with the women he held two retreats, and this was the burden of a sermon he preached there:

Social timidity is the sad proof that millions of baptized persons no longer fully trust the vested clergy with their alleged office of forgiveness and reconciliation. What then is the use of our single-track theology and philosophy if it continues to make the philosopher pass by on the other side while here, on this side of the road to Jericho, all sorts of fallen men and women are in the hands of the robbers, seducers, and all their fashionable fellow-travelers? For the pilgrim there is no early withdrawal to the Levite's ivory tower.

If you ask me what a pilgrim's truthful attitude should be, I would answer that a pilgrim's serenity is but a child's simplicity. If you give up all your mind's sophistication, your haughty professionalism, then people by the wayside will not hurry away so shocked and shamefaced as soon as you undertake to talk on Christian life.

It is we in the church who have often made the derivative term Christian an ambiguous one. But it is Christ who sets our standards right. He does it, if only we reaffirm that the whole of our life is his. For we cannot have any kind of fruitful living together outside the fellowship of his love.

Thus the undaunted pilgrim concerned himself with seeking and saving those who were labeled "lost" in the sight of the pretentious wardens of traditional rigidity. He was also to exert his influence on behalf of hundreds of thousands who were just at the age of fourteen to fifteen years. In unanimous action his synod held the young people back from swearing an oath of allegiance to the cause of world revolution. In no country of the huge Soviet orbit was the world philosophy of Marxism and Leninism so thoroughly and even religiously operated as in Otto Dibelius' diocese and, in fact, in the whole zone which the rulers of the Kremlin allowed to be called the sovereign German Democratic Republic. It was this quasi-religious side of the totalitarian power which he found he could not tolerate, at least not in the area entrusted to his pastoral care:

In a way, we may thank God's providence that ours is now the nation in which the issues are reaching right down into the uttermost depths of human existence. If now we are graced with strength and wisdom enough to preserve our children from giving their young souls away, surrendering their future to the uniform pattern of animal-like existence, then we may also render a good Samaritan's service to people in other nations of the West.

Among the eastern satellites, there are no such elaborate rites of initiation as we have in East Germany's state-supported feasts of communist youth induction. In our own area where East meets West, the terrific and sad experiment is made with every possible amount of vigor and enforcement.

Whether he lives in the East or in the West, he would be of the hireling type of leader indeed who could feel indifferent to the host of prospective newcomers to the communist camp. The young sheep now speeded through the widely open gate were persons indeed, children born to be free, brothers of Christ however young and inexperienced. If the deity of the uniform state wanted their souls, the church was there to rise and remind a weary fellowship that the Lord's grace is sufficient for each of them, for his power is made perfect in weakness.

We may not have nor, indeed, require any political means to stop the enforced process of attuning young German Protestants to the communist dialectic. Yet the responsibility for each young man's and each young woman's design, the care for his and her existence as a human person, is given to the family of Christ.

I am nothing more than just one of the fathers in that family. But no power on earth can take away my commitment, interwoven with my responsibility, when once each of these young persons has been named after Christ and the new name has been written down in the Book of Life.

The year was 1956. Thousands of specially trained propagandists and leaders of the communist youth organization were let loose on half a million adolescents whose names were still not struck off the churches' baptismal registers. Berlin's bishop presented not only the children, but also all of their parents with these challenging questions:

What does Christian baptism mean to you? Is it nothing more than a memory of a more or less pleasant family festival? Does sponsorship with a godfather's vow represent just one more of those dusty museum pieces which have made bogus both your goodly heritage and your family's pledge for the future which is founded on the sacred vow of your marriage? Is the sacramental side of human partnership forever ignored? Or is sponsorship being at last re-envisaged as that holy steward-ship which may enrich your unabated and unutterable task in life? Do not grieve God's holy spirit whose seal you bear until the day of your redemption dawns (Ephesians 4:30).

What does confirmation mean to you? Is it also just an oc-casion for hailing the excitation of adolescent feeling coincid-ing with the end of a child's innocence, as our pagan ancestors rejoiced in a man's youthful independence, early lust, and self-satisfaction? Or is confirmation an entering into blessed com-munion, a starting-point for a life committed to the Christ-giv-en reality, sealing each child's eternal dependence on the Father who performed the prior act of loving and hallowing each man's offspring? Are we to forget that it is our glorious birthright to hallow the times that are given to us on this earth? After the Creator's prior act we can draw a great consequence for all our earthly life. We can respond wholeheartedly as loving children do. Such a response will bring about the new creation. In the coming new order of a creation restored to the Maker's image faith, hope, and love will rise to become the determining fac-tors in our making of history.

Shall we ever abandon the blessed experience of our fellow-ship in the cells and catacombs, the partaking of a community greater and deeper than all the bonds of political expediency? Is not our brave Fellowship of the Young, our solid minority of the confirmed resisters, in reality a fellowship of loving con-cern, more lasting than all the imposing structures built by tem-poral necessity?

In the youth groups of tens and twenties, we have the very covenanters who have made their decision with Christ and for his cause, thus joyfully overcoming the communist decree that outside the registered church service hours Christians must not assemble in any conspicuous number. Neither mass organiza-tion nor mass psychology can fully compete with the decisive factor of mankind's promised transmutation. That ultimate factor is surely God's love joyfully responded to by New Man.

Would our youth groups and their unpretentious leaders have become the object of a state persecution now lasting well over three years were they not rightly seen as what they are in spite of the smallness of their numbers? Indeed they are the makers of a new history. Or would you think their historic mission is over when they have died in their cells or isolation camps?

These questions were all keenly listened to. A wholesome reconsideration of baptism and confirmation and indeed of all the church family's sacramental life was that year's sure harvest. When confirmation time was over, the communist-controlled press of Germany published a statement that in 1956 the number of baptized young persons who had registered for confirmation was considerably smaller than it had been in 1955. The actual difference was four per cent. In a country retaining several features of the tradition of the national church of which each person became a member at birth, four is a small percentage. In quality, the loss of those sheep was more than made up by a nationwide reassessment of the sacraments and their meaning for everyday life.

The churchman who was called a guardian of faith and hope in western civilization's most disputed eastern outpost came to be seen as a very human person whose independence from secular forces and influences was the mellowing fruit of a life lived in a child's utter dependence on the Father.

A true child is seldom at rest, and fellow-pilgrims have often discovered in Otto Dibelius a divine restlessness. A true child is not in despair, even if he sometimes suffers from the inadequacy of his powers. Before Christmas services and carol-singing were forbidden in eastern Stalinstadt (in 1955), the Bishop would spend Christmas Eve in a workmen's barracks there. These were his words:

> I came here to your barracks because I love the German worker too much to deny him the message of joy on Christmas Eve. But it doesn't matter whether or not my feelings for you in the barracks are to be requited. You know the proverb, "If I love you, what is it to you?" Love is my own

pledge, my adventurous task. The pledge and the venture of love—I will exercise it in all the imperfection which is my portion in life, and I will stay with you as long as you can stand my words of love passed on from heaven.

A strong child is not easily satisfied by what the outside world may have to offer. Fellow-workers have derived an untold inspiration from Otto Dibelius' divine discontent, his continued contravention of a history seen and operated without Christ. Visitors from East and West alike have come to realize what the Bishop's rejection of the successive kinds of secular government achieved as a positive result: on the interzonal island of Berlin, in the quadripartite heart of the much-disputed capital, an inner island was created providing an atmosphere of protection and safety. A deepened sense of human neighborhood and responsible stewardship was the blessed fruit of fervent prayers and quiet labors on this strange and rocky island.

In a completely divided country, the Bishop's continued ministry to East as well as West has kept alive the fine feeling of togetherness in spirit and culture, a feeling solid enough to serve as a reliable basis for discussing and acting together across the deadly political frontiers with reference to the prepolitical questions of human existence.

A genuine child does not reply to everyone who faces him with a strict and sudden command, or with a majority vote. To censor or punish such a child is seldom a profitable undertaking. Parliamentarians have been at a loss to reconcile the Bishop's acceptance of a quiet martyrdom with his critical attitude toward various ways in which democratic power has come to be exercised. Not that he followed London's gloomy Dean Inge's description of twentieth century churches as the newly appointed court chaplains to King Demos. He was more concerned with a positive manifestation of God's initiative in history. He found the question times in parliaments and convocations always stimulating. Yet he would not like to have them confused with the acceptable hour at which God raises his ultimate questions as to man's place in history:

To be ready for listening to God's challenging voice re-
quires a lifetime of preparation. But he speaks to every one of
us already.

For the people wholeheartedly concerned with the restoring
of man's heavenly image, it has often been a comfort to notice
their leader's genuine dislike for long and dreary synod meetings at which even the affirmative votes are cast in a spirit of
friction and in an atmosphere of vacillation. His office was of a
different character; it was to be firm and prophetic, an office
exercised with the holy passion of a person completely dependent on the living God.

One of his Asian friends of the Middle East has rightly
pointed out that "at mid-century already this island city church
of Berlin appears to stand out as a radiant cornerstone of the
coming realm of Christ." In an era seemingly occupied with
schemes for earthly destruction, Dibelius has made it impossible for East and West alike to ignore the Church of Christ
now reunited for constructive world service and integrated as a
factor in history.

A loving child can easily forget earlier hardships and failures.
Members of Dibelius' church, clerical and lay alike, have come
to marvel at the superior way in which their own true shepherd
valiantly overcame the preoccupation of pharisaic folk with the
envenomed consequences of unforgiven sins. A man of prayer,
he firmly and quietly superseded the allergic way in which the
sick-minded and the sophisticated are so often absorbed by the
bargaining over unsettled conflicts. In their appointed Pastor
and Bishop hundreds of thousands have come to recognize a
living instrument of healing and godly sharing. His "portion in
life" has been to wrestle with living truth rather than to build
back awe-inspiring power positions founded on issues doomed
to die. With that portion was associated the sacred pledge to
make the holy church a more human affair than it had been in
the centuries before. Harmonizing his truly apostolic mission
with wide participation in the church's cultural and spiritual
affairs, he has helped to make the peoples of all continents

aware of their ultimate alternative: they can be fellow-laborers with God to make this century a century of his fellowship and love, or else they can make this century the very last of human life.

Facing up victoriously to totalitarian claims of this world, dealing justly with the growing forces of secularism and soul-destroying Marxist materialism, Germany's spiritual leader has never stressed the negative character of church resistance. With him, the church is always at a higher level than the parties in political contention. Even far behind the zonal barriers and curtains, the essential life of Christian communities continues.

Long before the life of this child of the Father was to come to full fruition, his holy commitment presented the world with a two-fold achievement, and also with an undiluted source of joy and hope: a safeguarding of western man's sacred inheritance and a redemptive anticipation of the coming day's reality, the fellowship of God with man—warmly, lovingly, humanly restored through Him who came to seek what was lost.

Appendix

Bishop Otto Dibelius' Broadcast in London on the Occasion of Professor Karl Barth's 70th Birthday on May 10, 1956

It was not at all easy for us to establish good relations with Karl Barth, who is now celebrating his 70th birthday in Basle. When I say "us" I mean my generation, the men who are his age or a little older, most of whom no longer walk on this earth. In 1929 Adolf Harnack at whose feet all of us had sat wrote to Martin Rade, saying he never would have thought that he, Harnack, who was renowned for his gift of understanding alien trends of thought, would live to see speculation developing in Germany for which he had no antenna. He simply did not understand the mentality which governed Barth's writing. None of us understood it.

I remember exactly what I felt when in 1920 I opened his *Epistle to the Romans* which had recently been published. *The Epistle to the Romans*—that was the title, nothing more. The great Epistle of St. Paul was treated chapter by chapter, passage by passage. Well, we were used to such books; we were used to the Greek text first being determined by exact philological methods, and then being conscientiously translated, and we were used to every verse being carefully weighed as to what the writer could have meant—where his ideas might have an historical background, and where he was original, and so forth. That is what we expected when we took up a book with the title *The Epistle to the Romans*.

But of all these things there was nothing in this book. Instead the author poured dogmatics over the Epistle. It was a dogmatic that was strange to us. But that was not the worst. Why shouldn't someone write an uncommon dogmatic? Possibly this one did the fundamental conception of the Epistle more justice than other dogmatics. But that it claimed to be a commentary, that it occasionally took the liberty of giving a translation that the text did not permit, that ideas were interpreted into the text which the apostle could not possibly have had in this context, that over and over again the book claimed to be an exposition of the Epistle, whereas it was really only the author's own dogmatic concept—all this was offensive.

It was contrary to everything we had been brought up on. I read 20 pages, I read 40 pages, I read 60 pages. But after that I shut the book, resolved never to open it again.

Then came the sermons which Barth published together with his colleague Thurneysen. What sermons they were! Practically with no psychological consideration of the hearer, no respect of time, no connection with the life of the world. They were theological sermons each of which could just as well have been preached at Christmas as on All Souls' Day. Nowhere was there a word of simple moral exhortation, as after all is to be found in the Epistles, and we would not want to miss in modern preaching. Certainly we had no use for sermons of this kind.

The whole one-sidedness and vigor of Karl Barth was alien to us. With him theological thinking had become a form of existence in comparison with which everything else appeared secondary and unimportant. We too had a very high respect for theological learning, and we too were of the opinion that whoever had not studied theology could not really understand the spiritual bacground of life in the past and the present. However, *Theologische Existenz*—"theological existence"—the idea that theological thinking meant life itself was new to us.

And then Karl Barth had expressed political opinions by which he offended us. Karl Barth had become famous in Germany and through Germany. His international reputation had been founded during the years he had taught as professor in Göttingen, Münster, and Bonn. Nevertheless he was Swiss, and we found it arrogant of him to comment on political matters in Germany, and to criticize in the sharp way he did, things which were our national concern. A foreigner, we thought, should be more reticent in his judgment of a nation which had received him as a guest. We were angry with Karl Barth.

The young generation obviously did not take this view. We were astonished to see how the young people warmed toward him. Now his books were published in numbers which had been unknown in theological publication in Germany for years. The "Barthian School" became an institution; it began to win over the church. But we—we just couldn't follow.

And then came the time of National Socialism. Karl Barth could no longer hold his place in Germany and returned to Switzerland. But the eyes of the younger generation were still turned to him. It was this young generation which at the time joined in the struggle of the Confessing Church. The older generation was not completely absent, but the young dominated it. These younger ones seldom resented Karl Barth's political utterances. In this passionate opposition to the nationalist hysteria of Adolf Hitler they had to some degree lost the natural, unquestioned patriotism of former times. They had no objection to a man from Switzerland criticizing Germany.

And "theological existence" was just the thing for the young generation. The institutions which had hitherto been regarded as the practical proof of Christian faith—the home and foreign missions and other similar activities could not develop within the National Socialist totalitarian state. They could only exist in the background and wait for better times. And so it became all the more the obligation of the church to fight the National

Socialist ideology. It was here that resistance had to be offered. The church could not be forbidden to preach, nor could one forbid theological teaching at schools and universities. Here was the place for witness, a witness which was different to that of the *Deutsche Christen* (German Christians); it had to be a definite theological witness, with no regard to things outside the church, or the events of the day, as this was not possible. The church needed advice, guidance, and help for this task, and so it took recourse to the books of Karl Barth.

Then in 1934, when the Synod of the Confessing Church in Barmen set out to formulate a fundamental declaration against the heresies of the time, Karl Barth was called to help. It was he who, with the cooperation of his German friends, formulated the "Theological Declaration of Barmen" which gave the Confessing Church its direction and guidance.

It was a theological declaration; it never became, nor could become, popular. But it was respected far beyond the circle of theologians. That it was criticized, and that this criticism often revealed a different "existential attitude," rather than theological thinking, does not alter the fact that this Theological Declaration constitutes a landmark in the recent history of the Protestant Church in Germany.

Henceforth we elder ones also regarded the life-work of Karl Barth with different eyes. We could not capitulate before his theological views. I could only name very few theologians of my age who became adherents of Karl Barth's theology. We were molded by the traditional way of thinking in which we had been trained, and we desired to see the proofs of Christian faith in deeds and actions. But we now realized two things: (1) that exactly in the year 1919, when Karl Barth's *Epistle to the Romans* was published, a new era of thinking had begun. The philosophy of existentialism had lifted its head. Interest in history was dying out. People were no longer interested in psychological examinations. The whole of the sermons by Rittelmeyer which were based on psychological considerations, and had played such a leading part in Germany before World War I, were suddenly unsaleable. Communism faced the world with

entirely new problems. "Dialectic thinking" became the common property of all intellectuals. Something new had begun.

And to this new thing, this spiritual revolution, belonged
Karl Barth's theology. That became clearer from year to year.
And we especially, who had been trained to think in historical
terms, knew what a revolution of this kind signified. We knew
that such changes did not depend on the actions and volitions
of men, but came over mankind from a higher power. We
knew that those who could not easily surrender to this new
thing were not necessarily barren reactionaries. Later times will
restore to honor again much that was genuine in their views.
But it would be futile to set oneself against the changing times.
In some way all of us are drawn into this change, whether we
realize it or not. This we knew, and we consented to accept
Karl Barth's theology as an expression of the new times.

(2) In the times of the church struggle it became evident
that Karl Barth's theology had given men the strength to resist
the heresies of the time, and it was not difficult to see why that
was so. Karl Barth called attention to the essential. He called
attention to the Word of God, radically and exclusively. He
despised Christian idealism with all it implied. With him it
was the Word of God, and nothing but the Word of God that
mattered.

This had significance for all of us. We had grown up in the
idea that Fichte's *Anweisungen zum seligen Leben* (Guide to
Eternal Life) was a Christian book, and that what Goethe had
said in the latter period of his life could be added unhesitat-
ingly to the New Testament as a fifth Gospel. Now our eyes
were definitely opened. Now the difference between the gospel
of the Bible and idealism as the esoteric religion of the educated classes became relentlessly clear. And that was what a
church needed, that now had to fight for its life against foreign
ideologies. For the gospel a man can give his life. He not only
can give it, but he *does* give it—does it today as he did nineteen
hundred years ago. But for Goethe . . . well, I need not con-
clude the sentence.

In this point Karl Barth has rendered us a decisive service, and it would be a bad thing if we were not grateful to him for it. And we are readier to be grateful than we would have been 37 years ago. Karl Barth is no longer the same man he was then. *Tempora mutantur et nos mutamur in illis*—the times change and we with them; that is as true of Karl Barth as of us. Many of us, especially those who live in the tradition of Martin Luther, still differ in opinion from the man we are celebrating in Basle. But we pay respect to his grand life-work, notably in his "dogmatics." In him we honor one of the most important and productive theological thinkers of the past hundred years, and we thank him for the great service he has rendered the Protestant Church in Germany. This church will add its congratulations to those of other churches all the world over at the celebration on the tenth of May. Such a thing has hardly ever happened before. But then, we are living in new times.

Index of Names